"So What Are You Going to Do with That?"

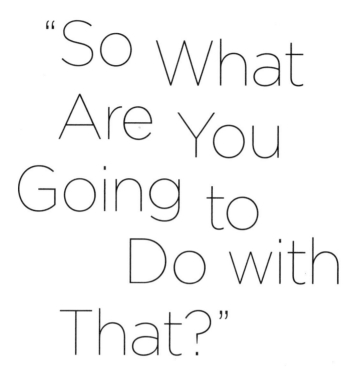

"So What Are You Going to Do with That?"

Finding Careers Outside Academia

REVISED EDITION

SUSAN BASALLA AND MAGGIE DEBELIUS

The University of Chicago Press   *Chicago and London*

Both Susan Basalla and Maggie Debelius earned their Ph.D.'s in English from Princeton University.

Susan Basalla writes regularly for the "Beyond the Ivory Tower" column in the *Chronicle of Higher Education* and, together with Maggie, gives talks on graduate student career options. She has worked in philanthropy, journalism, and new media, and is currently a managing associate for the Art & Science Group, which specializes in developing market-informed strategy for colleges and universities.

Maggie Debelius has taught writing and literature courses at the University of Colorado, Princeton, and Georgetown University and currently serves as the director of the Georgetown University Writing Center, where she trains faculty and students to teach writing. She also lectures across the country about career options for graduate students.

The University of Chicago Press, Chicago 60637
The University of Chicago Press, Ltd., London

This book was first published in 2001 by Farrar, Straus and Giroux under the title *"So What Are You Going to Do with That?": A Guide to Career-Changing for M.A.'s and Ph.D.'s.*
Revised edition published 2007
Printed in the United States of America

16 15 14 13 12 11 10 09 08 07   1 2 3 4 5

ISBN-13: 978-0-226-03881-0   (cloth)
ISBN-10: 0-226-03881-5   (cloth)

ISBN-13: 978-0-226-03882-7   (paper)
ISBN-10: 0-226-03882-3   (paper)

Library of Congress Cataloging-in-Publication Data

Basalla, Susan Elizabeth, 1970–
   "So what are you going to do with that?" : finding careers outside academia / Susan Basalla and Maggie Debelius. — Rev. ed.
      p.   cm.
   ISBN-13: 978-0-226-03881-0 (cloth : alk. paper)
   ISBN-10: 0-226-03881-5 (cloth : alk. paper)
   ISBN-13: 978-0-226-03882-7 (pbk. : alk. paper)
   ISBN-10: 0-226-03882-3 (pbk. : alk. paper)
   1. Job hunting.   2. Graduate students—Employment.   3. Career changes.   I. Debelius, Maggie, 1966–
II. Title.
   HF5382.7.B374   2007
   650.14—dc22

                                                        2006026038

♾ The paper used in this publication meets the minimum requirements of the American National Standard for Information Sciences—Permanence of Paper for Printed Library Materials, ANSI Z39.48-1992.

For my parents, with gratitude and love
For Greg, my favorite
S.B.

For Mike, Charlie, and Jack, who never make me question what
I want to do with my life. When I'm with them, I'm doing it.
M.D.

Contents

Preface

Five years after writing the first edition of this book, we believe more passionately than ever in the relevance of a Ph.D. or M.A. to careers outside the academy. The job market has changed since we wrote the first edition of "*So What Are You Going to Do with That?*" during the height of the Internet boom. But our message remains the same: We're more interested in helping people figure out a long-term career than a short-term job. You should do what will make you happy, regardless of market fluctuations.

While the substance of our work has not changed, we have updated the 2007 edition to include examples of graduate alumni in a wider range of careers. The original edition featured several Ph.D.'s working in technology companies; in this new edition, we've shifted our focus to include more of those working in government, academic administration, publishing, and other fields. We've also built a website (www.careersforphds.com) to consolidate some of the powerful Internet job-hunting resources geared specifically to academics and former academics.

After publishing the first edition, we heard from countless readers who told us that the book helped them see their talents and abilities in a new light. Some of these readers shared their stories with us as well as suggestions for improving the book. We are indebted to them and the other M.A.'s and Ph.D.'s who appear in the following pages for their generosity.

Introduction

So now what?

If you are now or have ever been a graduate student, you've heard the universal question about earning an M.A. or a Ph.D.: "So what are you going do with that? Teach?" One of the occupational hazards of academic life is enduring this kind of questioning from friends and family. Your least favorite uncle has probably called you overeducated and unemployable. And maybe, somewhere in the back of your mind, you also have occasional moments of doubt about your future: What *am* I going to do with my graduate degree?

Maybe you're halfway to graduation and suddenly wondering if teaching is the right career for you. Maybe your heart's not in it anymore; maybe you'd like to earn more money; maybe you'd like to live somewhere where there are few college-level teaching jobs. Or maybe, like increasing numbers of graduates, you'd love to teach but can't find a tenure-track job. With the market for college and university teaching jobs shrinking at an alarming rate, you need to consider all your options before, during, and after graduate school.

Or maybe you're a faculty member—tenured or otherwise—who's ready for a new way of life. Are you an academic nomad, traveling around the country from one adjunct position to another? Did your departmental review go badly and you just don't have the heart to seek another academic position? Or are you a tenured professor who can't face teaching the same courses and clashing with the same colleagues for one more semester? This book is for faculty as well as grad students. (In fact, we were surprised in our research to see how common it was for faculty to jump ship from academia.) You'll hear advice and anecdotes from many former professors in the chapters to come.

And scientists of all stripes, we're talking to you too. Conventional wisdom says that scientists have "hard skills" and therefore don't need any help with post-academic job hunting. But we know it's not always that easy, especially for people in sciences like biology and chemistry rather than engineering. You may have spent years enduring low pay and little independence in a postdoctoral position only to find that you're no closer to a tenure-track job. When you start to look for jobs outside academia, you may have trouble convincing employers that your intensive research on mouse digestive systems is relevant to their needs. And if you want to enter a field like consulting or law, how do you prepare yourself for life outside the laboratory? We have plenty of examples and advice for you as well.

Whether you are a grad student or professor, humanist or scientist, as academics you probably have one major trait in common: You feel like you'll never be able to reshape yourself into a real-world success after spending ten years studying one obscure topic. (Heck, you might not even own a suit.) We felt that way too. But, believe it or not, the same skills you need to succeed in academia—researching, writing, and teaching—will give you the edge in your job hunt. We will suggest a number of strategies to help you decide whether or not you want to continue going to graduate school, show you how to make the best use of your time while you're there, and teach you how to market yourself to employers after you leave. We'll show you everything you need to know to translate your academic credentials into a real-world job.

We've interviewed more than a hundred former graduate students and professors who have found challenging and fulfilling careers as everything from midwife to private investigator to television cooking show host to National Football League executive. We've also talked to people working happily in more traditional careers, such as editors, high school teachers, computer gurus, lawyers, university administrators, management consultants, entrepreneurs, and researchers. In the course of this book, we will introduce you to dozens of graduate alumni from the humanities, sciences, and social sciences, and explain exactly how they reached their goals. These alumni generously shared with us their advice, their anecdotes, and their secrets for success. They are all insightful, funny, inspiring, creative, and ambitious people—it was a joy to meet them. We've made their stories the heart of this book so you can learn as much from them as we did.

So Who Are We to Talk?

Since earning our degrees several years ago, we've both held a variety of jobs inside and outside the academy. We wrote the first edition of this book during the dot-com heyday, the boom years when unemployment was at an all-time low and starting salaries hit all-time highs. While those days are over, there are still plenty of opportunities outside academia for M.A.'s and Ph.D.'s who are willing to do the work required to land a post-academic job.

Susan's Story: Ph.D. English, Princeton University, 1997

I figured out that I didn't want to be a professor about halfway through my program, realizing one day that I just couldn't picture myself continuing to study the same narrow topic for the next decade. I had no idea what other kind of career would be open to me, but I knew that I wanted to finish my degree first. Luckily, my adviser was supportive and agreed to help me streamline my dissertation so I could finish quickly.

Although I was worried that my parents would be disappointed by my leaving academia, they were actually relieved. My father (a history professor) had seen too many graduate students cycle unsuccessfully through the job market year after year and didn't want me to suffer that way if I could be happy doing something else. Both of my parents offered to support me for a year so I could finish my dissertation without having to teach. I stocked up on Diet Coke and hummus and wrote as fast as I could. Having a deadline and knowing that I would never go on the academic job market made it much easier for me to just get it done.

During the year that I finished my dissertation, I also started researching other careers. The university career center didn't have many resources for graduate students then (that's no longer the case), and my department had little experience with the issue. Hoping to find someone who understood my situation, I got a list of English Ph.D.'s from the alumni office and started cold-calling people to ask for advice. (My department chair kindly helped me get the list, though in retrospect I realize that I could have asked the alumni office for it myself.) Much to my surprise, everyone I spoke to seemed happy and fulfilled in his or her new career and was more than willing to offer advice and contacts. Those early conversations were the germ of this book.

After I defended my dissertation, I asked the temp agency I'd worked for during summers and vacations to place me somewhere that I might be able to get hired full-time. They sent me to the Robert Wood Johnson Foundation, which turned out to be a great place for a Ph.D. Within a few months, I was hired as a full-time research assistant and began learning about health policy. When I decided that I wanted to move to Washington, D.C., I answered a classified ad and became a reporter for a medical newsletter just outside the city. My fellow reporters were all recent college grads, and my editor was several years younger than I was. I swallowed my pride and got to work. I soon found that the skills I'd learned in graduate school served me well as a reporter: I was able to absorb large amounts of complex information quickly and translate it into clear, plain English prose. I moved up quickly and never regretted starting at the bottom. I learned important skills along the way, and in my subsequent tour through the world of new media, I again found that my ability to learn quickly was my greatest asset.

After the first edition of this book came out in 2001, I began writing the "Beyond the Ivory Tower" column for the *Chronicle of Higher Education* and speaking to graduate students across the country about post-academic careers. For four years, I continued to write and speak about post-academic careers while working full-time for the Motley Fool and later for America Online. In 2004 a networking contact I'd made years before suddenly paid off. Back in 2002 I'd done an information interview with someone who worked in educational consulting. It sounded like a dream job to me, but her company was small and had no openings. However, when she needed to hire someone to replace her two years later, she called to see if I was still interested. Happily, I got the job and now feel that I've finally found the right career for me. My work is challenging and creative, my colleagues are smart and funny, and I'm allowed to bring my dog to the office. What more could I want? I even find that I do a lot of teaching in my job—particularly in the form of public speaking—and I enjoy it enormously. It turns out that having one foot in academia is enough for me. I love working with universities because I care about their mission, but I know that I can serve them better in my current role than I ever could have as a faculty member.

Maggie's Story: Ph.D. in English, Princeton University, 2000

Throughout graduate school, I straddled the fence between the academic and post-academic worlds by working as a freelance writer. I loved teaching but struggled to find my voice as an academic writer. Journalism provided me with both a paycheck and a reminder that I could write—even when I couldn't face my dissertation. I took some time off from the dissertation entirely to work as an editor for an Internet company in the late '90s. Like many of those we interviewed, taking a break from writing proved beneficial for me. My employer allowed me to work four days a week, I wrote my dissertations on Fridays and weekends, and I ended up being much more productive than when I tried to write full-time.

My own writing struggles have led me back to the academy, where I now work as director of the Writing Center at Georgetown University in Washington, D.C. This position puts me just where I want to be: at the crossroads of the academy and the rest of the world. I teach in the English department, train the Georgetown students who staff the Writing Center, and work with writers at all stages of the composing process. I also get to work with writers who face some of the same obstacles that I did when writing my dissertation.

I consider myself fortunate to continue to straddle the academic and post-academic divide: this position allows me to do the teaching I love and also gives me the chance to consider connections between my students' academic writing and the other writing that they do. I also have time to pursue freelance writing jobs as well as to conduct training in writing for non-academic audiences. Soon after I took the job, I began to receive numerous calls from local companies seeking writing instruction for their employees. A manager from the World Bank wanted to teach her employees to be more concise. A caller from Freddie Mac needed help getting his people to write as a team. A scientist knew his postdocs would qualify for more grants if only they could learn to summarize their interesting research more effectively. Initially I turned these callers away because I barely had the time or resources to work with my own students and handle the administrative responsibilities of running the center. After a year or two in the job, however, it occurred to me that these occasional calls were an opportunity rather than an intrusion. I joined forces with a colleague in the Georgetown English department to launch a company that specializes in teaching on-site writing seminars for businesses. The workshop techniques and editing exercises that have become staples in writing classrooms across the country have proved valuable to and effective for several companies we've worked with.

So for me the barrier between the academic and post-academic worlds continues to be a permeable one. It doesn't have to be an either/or decision. Just as I continued to publish in academic journals while working full-time as a website editor, so likewise I continue to work as a freelance journalist and corporate trainer while working full-time at Georgetown. Rather than feeling my life is split into two halves, I feel my interests complement each other. Working outside the academy makes me a better teacher, because I can share a broad base of experience with my students (and help them job-hunt when necessary). And my academic work informs all the post-academic writing and teaching that I do, helping me adapt the best of the classroom to the workplace. Five years after writing the first edition of this book, I believe more passionately than ever in the relevance of a Ph.D. or an M.A. to careers outside the academy.

So What's This Book All About?

This book evolved from a series of late-night phone calls in which we questioned our future prospects and self-worth. What would our friends say if we left the profession? What would our advisers think? Our parents? Our spouses? Like many graduate students who contemplate careers outside academia, we felt a little sheepish—as though, after years of academic success, we had failed the ultimate test: getting a tenure-track job. And even though we weren't exactly sure what we wanted for ourselves, we began researching careers outside academia. In the process, we discovered a stunning collection of smart, successful, and satisfied M.A.'s and Ph.D.'s.

Because we'd never known these renegade Ph.D.'s existed during our years in graduate school, we decided to collect their narratives in one place. All too often we've heard friends seeking jobs as professors announce, "I just can't imagine doing anything else." Of course they can't—many of them came straight from college and have been in grad school for the last decade. And this book is for them—to help them imagine other lives.

With that goal in mind, we're using the term "post-academic" careers instead of "non-academic" or "alternative" careers, because we want to banish the notion that there is academia . . .

and then everything else. Academia is one choice among millions, although we often lose that perspective after spending years surrounded by people who've chosen identical careers.

In all our research, our most surprising discovery was that few post-academics completely abandon their academic interests. Rather, they find creative ways to continue a trajectory that started long before graduate school. Instead of making a U-turn in the middle of their lives, most of these alumni followed up on a lifelong interest or a half-forgotten talent by traveling a parallel path toward an equally fulfilling destination. Throughout this book, we will show you again and again the unexpected ways in which these alumni use their academic training in their new careers and the surprising connections between their academic interests and their post-academic careers.

So What Are We Supposed to Do Now?

The story Stacey Rees shared with us illustrates how your academic research can lead you, unexpectedly, to a post-academic career. Rees left Princeton's comparative literature Ph.D. program after her fifth year. She now works as a nurse-midwife in New York City. Here's the tale of how and why she made that leap.

Rees wasn't making very speedy progress on her dissertation; her subject was the image of motherhood in French medieval literature. She had taken on several part-time jobs during graduate school, including one at a birthing center. She began to realize over the course of a year or two that she enjoyed her part-time job more than she enjoyed her graduate school work. She started to suspect that she was in graduate school primarily because she had been a good student as an undergraduate—a case of sheer momentum. Her part-time jobs were a way of subconsciously undercutting her own progress.

Over the next six months, she thought hard about what had been important to her before she came to graduate school, what made her happy now, and what she wanted her life to be in the future. While visiting a friend who was training to be an obstetrician and spending all day talking with her about women's health, Rees woke up that morning at 3 a.m., sat up straight in bed, and said, "I want to be a midwife!" Few of us will be blessed with that kind of epiphany (and even fewer with that *particular* epiphany), but for Rees, it was born of weeks of soul-searching about what she wanted her future to look like.

The first time an academic friend of ours heard this story, he said, "So? Now we're all supposed to go be midwives?" Obviously not. But his response is a great example of what we call the "Plan B" dilemma. We've all been training for exactly the same job as assistant professor, so when post-academic careers come up, the first question is "What do *we all* do next?"—as if there can be a universal Plan B that will accommodate all of us. As Rees's story shows, the decision is—and must be—highly personal.

Rees uses her graduate school skills every day. She calls herself a born teacher and knows she would miss the classroom if she gave it up completely. But as a midwife, instead of teaching undergraduates, she teaches mothers—one-on-one and in groups—at a critical point in their lives. About her research skills, she says:

> Midwifery demands that you continually update your skills, and you must be able to comfortably consult, weigh, and evaluate current research. Graduate school made me comfortable with taking on the experts, so to speak. I left grad school with a tendency toward reading critically, which is especially important for supporting the practice of midwifery since it often flies in the face of conventional obstetrical wisdom.

Since leaving graduate school, she has published several academic articles, something she never did as a grad student. Rees also credits her graduate school training with two other important transferable skills. Her familiarity with academic scholarship won her a part-time editorial job with the *Journal of the*

American Medical Women's Association, and her foreign-language training makes it possible for her to work abroad someday.

What we find so compelling about Rees's story is that, rather than imagining herself as "nothing but" an expert on an esoteric topic, she took from her dissertation an awareness of her lifelong interests. Instead of laboring over her dissertation and experiencing that awful "What else could I possibly do?" postpartum depression, Rees turned that process inside out. Her dissertation on motherhood gave birth to a midwife.

As every graduate student knows, your dissertation topic is a mini–Rorschach test of your personality. It's great cocktail party conversation to psychoanalyze people based on their choice to study, say, Marilyn Monroe rather than Emily Dickinson. But in order to imagine a life outside academia, you'll need to open up that process, as Rees did, and figure out what your dissertation, and your graduate school experience as a whole, has taught you about yourself.

Another reason we like Rees's story is that it explodes some of the most prevalent myths about post-academic careers. The myths about what graduate students can and can't do, what employers do and don't want, are extremely powerful. Debunking these myths is one of our major reasons for writing a career guide just for academics. As one former economics grad student cited in a *Chronicle of Higher Education* article put it: "Graduate school is the academic equivalent of Parris Island. The fact that . . . boot camp demoralizes you does not mean you are not capable." We went through the same basic training and can tell you that shaking that mind-set is the most important step you can take toward a satisfying life outside academia. If you believe that you have somehow failed your higher purpose, you will never be happy outside academia, no matter what job you find.

Sharyl Nass, a Ph.D. in cell and tumor biology, found this fear of failure to be one of the biggest barriers to exploring jobs outside the academy. For her, the move was "agonizing" because "my scientific mentors told me I was throwing my career away" by leaving the academy. "There is incredible bias and ar-

rogance in academia with regard to 'alternate' careers in science," she explains. But since finishing a postdoctoral fellowship at Johns Hopkins University and moving to a health policy position at the Institute of Medicine, she has found real satisfaction rather than imagined failure. She now uses her knowledge to advise the White House on issues surrounding cancer treatment and prevention.

Another scientist, Shannon Mrksich, recalls explaining to her parents that she wouldn't be wasting her doctorate in chemistry by becoming a patent attorney. "Helping resolve biotechnology patent disputes is another way of helping to cure cancer," she remembers telling them. "People always say, 'You've spent your whole life doing this, and now you're throwing it all away,'" Mrksich says. "But they never think to say, 'What a great stepping-stone to other things.'"

So What Can Universities Do?

Numerous studies have shown that only a small percentage of doctoral students become tenure-track professors at a research institution. In their 1999 study, "Ph.D.'s—10 Years Later," Maresi Nerad and Joseph Cerny found that only 58 percent of Ph.D.'s in English were on the tenure track or tenured ten years after graduation. Of those, only 16 percent worked at top research universities (*Communicator,* Fall 1999).

The reality of too many candidates and not enough faculty positions has led to considerable anger among graduate students. Their anger at Ph.D. underemployment has been directed at professional associations, university administrators, and other similar targets. Since we published the first edition of this book in 2001, many graduate institutions across the country have responded to the job shortage by developing "Preparing Future Professionals" programs to introduce their students to a wide variety of careers. While we applaud these efforts, we also know there's more work to be done. Many universities have invested resources in graduate career counselors, but few have been able to effect change at the departmental level. Until faculty and administrators overcome a prejudice against careers in the business, government, and nonprofit sectors, graduate students will continue to dismiss potentially satisfying careers for fear of adviser and departmental disapproval. Here are a few steps we'd like to see departments take:

- Department chairs and deans could track and assess the careers of all their Ph.D.'s and M.A.'s—not just for one to two years after completion and not only for those who enter academia, but for five to ten years and for all who enter the program. Publish the results of this survey prominently to communicate the value of successful careers in a variety of fields.
- Create an e-mail Listserv of graduate alumni employed outside the academy who are willing to talk to students about their career choices.
- Invite graduates employed outside the academy to speak about their work in a colloquium setting, just as they do with their professoriate alumni.

In addition to these practical steps, we would like departments to reconsider their silent (and sometimes quite vocal) disapproval of post-academic careers. Too many graduate students hide their post-academic career searches from their advisers and dissertation committees for fear of being unjustly labeled failures. Shaming a student into an unwanted academic career helps no one. As Ms. Mentor, whose column on academic life appears regularly in the *Chronicle of Higher Education*, explains:

> Disappointing one's adviser, fearing one's adviser, dwelling with the dread that others may know that one has "real world" interests . . . Ms. Mentor is reminded of the astute comment by Shug Avery, Alice Walker's super-cool and feisty character in *The Color Purple*: "Why any woman would give a shit what people think is a mystery to me."
>
> Ms. Mentor takes the comment to refer to both genders, and

admits that often graduate students have gotten where they are—
to Ph.D. programs—by giving many a shit about what people
think. . . . This is a not a bad thing. Ms. Mentor was, of course,
always a superb student.

Because most graduate students care so much about earning approval, an adviser's casual comment about a past student who
has "left the profession," made in disparaging tones, can carry
far more weight than intended. Considering that, as Ms. Mentor points out, "as of 2005, only 40 percent of Ph.D.'s in English
were getting tenure-track jobs, and only 30 percent of Ph.D.'s
in history," it is irresponsible of departments to denigrate a
choice that, by necessity, a large number of students are forced
to make.

And What Can You Do?

While universities need to make changes, those changes won't
happen quickly enough to improve your prospects if you are a
grad student or professor today. Without absolving universities of responsibility, we believe that it is counterproductive to
rage against a deeply rooted problem while accumulating enormous personal debt, both literally and figuratively. Ms. Mentor
cautions against allowing fear of disappointing one's adviser to
limit one's choices:

> Caring desperately what others think—valuing the "Dr." in
> one's name—and thinking that academe is only a higher calling,
> and not a business can lead people to be bitter and to give away
> some of their best years, when they could be developing a busi-
> ness, working for nonprofits, writing for politicians, researching
> for the public good. Teaching is not the only way to be socially
> or intellectually useful, and many [other careers] pay better.
>
> Ms. Mentor would like humanities Ph.D. students to put
> themselves first and to worry most about pleasing themselves
> with sufficient money and abundant self-respect for their own
> gifts and talents. Many advisers want to replicate themselves,

> but Alice Student is not Dr. Adviser's clone. In everyone's life, their own shit has to come first.

We couldn't agree more. At its heart, this book is designed to help you make the most of your gifts and talents—in whatever arena you choose to work.

We're not suggesting that post-academic careers are the magic-bullet solution to the current job crisis. But whatever reforms are instituted may be too late to help those who are currently unable to find full-time teaching positions. We're here to say that you have a choice. If you decide that you want or need to leave academia for economic, geographical, family, or other reasons, we can help you figure out another path to happiness, security, and intellectual fulfillment.

Not a single person we interviewed regretted leaving academia. While some acknowledged missing certain aspects of academic life, they found compensatory virtues in their post-academic careers. A few alums who deeply loved teaching told us that they would consider returning to some kind of college-level teaching again in the future, but only on their own terms—as one option among many other jobs—not with the kind of desperation that a rookie academic brings to the job market. Other studies confirm this trend: the English Ph.D.'s surveyed by Nerad and Cerny who were employed outside the academy reported overall job satisfaction that was equal to or higher than their colleagues employed in tenured and tenure-track jobs.

We recognize that our enthusiasm about post-academic careers could be mistaken for naive optimism. Critics of "alternative" careers have remarked that graduate students who have spent years preparing to be scholars don't want to settle for boring office jobs. But your fate is in your hands. If you want interesting work, you must devote yourself to finding it. If you think that you can't possibly be happy outside academia, you probably won't be.

We understand that academia is a way of life—we felt the pain of leaving the fold—but believe us, the pain does not last.

We understand that being forced to leave a career you love because of a weak job market is heartbreaking. But does that mean you should continue miserably treading water?

Let's look at your options. What are you supposed to do if you don't get a job the moment that you finish your dissertation? (And let's face it, who does?) You're supposed to take a one-year job or a postdoctoral fellowship in order to patch together an income—and, God willing, some health insurance—while you wait for a tenure-track position. But we all know the sad truth is that the longer you spend adjuncting, the less likely you are to land that rare tenure-track job. And in the sciences, one postdoc may just lead to another. You may become unfairly marked as somehow undesirable. And sadly, it's often the most devoted teachers and scholars who endure low pay and crummy working conditions in hopes of a long-term payoff. "Adjuncts may be doing the best teaching of anyone in the academy," writes Ms. Mentor. "But they should not do it forever."

So here's our radical proposal: Why not get a post-academic job while you wait out the market? You can shrink the pool of willing adjunct teachers and postdoctoral fellows. You can earn twice as much money at a job that doesn't consume your life the way academia does. You can live where you want to live— maybe even in the same state as your spouse or partner. You can work nine to five and use your free time to teach a class on the side if you like. You can start knocking down your mounting credit card debt, prepare yourself for another career, and take back some power for yourself. And when the market comes around again, you may decide that you're happy where you are. And if you do decide to go back on the market, it'll be on your own terms. You'll be a stronger and more confident candidate for having proven yourself in the outside world—plus, you won't feel pressured to take any academic job that's offered.

Yes, we know it's not that easy and that there are serious risks in walking away from the "pure" academic track. But we propose that you consider the possibility—even if just for a moment—as an alternative to spending yet another year as an adjunct. In the face of so much despair about what Ph.D.'s can and can't do with their lives, we are willing to err on the side of optimism. We're here to say that as intimidating as the process appears at first, there is a universe of possibilities open to you. This is the beginning of a new phase in your life—a chance for you to find out something unexpected about yourself.

What You'll Find in This Book

Chapter 1—"Will I Have to Wear a Suit?"—will help you assess your current situation and gain some perspective on what a post-academic career might offer you. Figuring out what you want to do, rather than what you're supposed to do, is the crucial first step. If you're in a rut trying to finish a project for which you (or your adviser) have lost enthusiasm, we can show you how to experiment with other fields without burning bridges behind you. We will debunk a few myths about post-academic careers and share advice from alums who've been there. We'll also address some of the psychological baggage that comes with the decision to explore careers outside the academy. This chapter will also show you how to make the best use of your grad school years by gaining new kinds of experiences on and off campus.

Chapter 2—"How Do I Figure Out What Else to Do?"—will introduce you to some self-evaluation exercises designed especially for graduate students. Before you start career shopping, you have to develop a general idea of what kind of career suits you best. Aimlessly trying on labels like "systems analyst," "pastry chef," or "hotshot lawyer" will only end up frustrating you if you don't know what your own limits are. The chapter ends with an overview of the industries to which academics seem drawn, along with profiles of alums working within those fields.

Chapter 3, "Testing the Waters," will help you to conduct your own research about fields that interest you through networking and information interviewing. In addition, we'll share the secrets of successful internships, part-time jobs, and volunteer work, which can give you in-depth access to a person or an industry.

Chapter 4, "This Might Hurt a Bit: Turning a CV into a Résumé," tackles one of the toughest obstacles facing former graduate students. Reorganizing your carefully developed curriculum vitae can be a painful and difficult experience. We'll help you figure out how to put your best foot forward without feeling like a sellout. We'll also show you résumés from real-life job seekers so you can see for yourself how they translated their academic skills into desirable commodities for an employer.

Chapter 5, "Sweaty Palms, Warm Heart," will prepare you for those nerve-racking interviews. You only have one shot with most employers, and you need to know how to sell your skills before you set foot in their offices. What do you say about your time in academia? How do you convince them you can do a job you've never done before? We'll combine specialized alumni advice with general interviewing tips to give you the confidence you need to win the job. Then we'll suggest how to negotiate your terms.

To keep all of this career hunting in perspective, in the conclusion we'll look at the bigger picture. What if you still aren't sure what you want to do? What if you hate your first job? Finally, you'll hear from academics who've had long careers outside universities and can offer some important advice.

It's gut-wrenching to change careers. It takes chutzpah. But it can also turn out to be the best thing you've ever done.

1 Will I Have to Wear a Suit?

Rethinking Life After Graduate School

Hearing that there is a universe of post-academic careers open to you can be more intimidating than reassuring. Following the academic track into an assistant professorship at least offers the comfort of a clearly defined path and plenty of fellow travelers. But if you venture outside academia, you are on your own. You may not even know anyone who works in the "real world." How are you supposed to decide where you belong?

While people in all kinds of professions wish for a clearer view of the career path ahead, graduate students and faculty members face some obstacles particular to academia. There's peer pressure from other academics, who think that leaving the profession means "failure"; there's personal and family angst over the large amount of time and money you've spent earning an advanced degree; and there's an annual job market that means long waits between job-hunting attempts. Whether you're 100 percent or only 10 percent sure that you should be in academia, taking a little time to explore what else is out there will help ensure that your choice is informed by desire, not habit or tradition.

We don't want to talk you out of an academic career—it may be exactly the right choice for you, and the professorial life has some wonderful benefits. But since there are so few voices out there to support those who are a little unsure, a little curious, or just plain stuck, we want to be your guides to exploring the other possibilities.

You might accuse us of glamorizing life outside academia. But, hey, we live out here—we know perfectly well that some days are miserable, some bosses are unbearable, and some jobs are just plain awful. But instead of emphasizing the negative, we've chosen to tell you about people who've worked their way through a maze of sometimes boring, usually low-level jobs to land in careers that are just right for them. And if we tell you about people who've succeeded against long odds, then it should be all the easier for you to picture yourself landing a "not perfect but a step in the right direction" kind of job.

Whatever you decide to do with your future, we want you to make a conscious choice. Former Columbia University English professor John Romano points out that while academic careers are considered to be the "safe" road to take after graduate school, the traditional approach carries more consequences than most Ph.D.'s realize. "Following tradition and taking that job at a small college in rural Nebraska is as risky as anything you do outside academia," he explains. In his own career, Romano turned down a job at a well-respected university because he feared its rural, small-town environment would cut off his escape routes to other careers. Romano advises current academics to remember that "it's too easy to drift into academia, but at the same time, drifting into it is also making a choice. . . . The fact that you are good at one thing doesn't mean you have to do it for the rest of your life. You may be good at other things, too, and never know it."

Romano himself took a big chance when he decided to leave Columbia to try a screenwriting career in Hollywood. Instead of writing the book that he needed to get tenure, Romano wrote a screenplay and began sending it out to movie studios. While the move was risky both personally (he had a wife and young child) and professionally, Romano's gamble paid off; he made it to Hollywood, where he's written for both movies and television. He credits Charles Dickens—the subject of his dissertation— with helping him understand how to write the twentieth century's version of popular serial fiction. Some of his career highlights include writing and producing such shows as *Hill Street Blues, Party of Five,* and *Monk.*

Getting Your Head Ready

We've given talks to graduate students at a number of universities since this book was first published, and in doing so we've learned that the greatest obstacle to a Ph.D.'s employment outside academia lies inside his or her own head. The emotional and psychological issues that leaving academia conjures up for most graduate students are a far greater barrier than employer indifference or lack of relevant skills. Leo Simonetta, a Ph.D. in social psychology and former faculty member who now works outside the academy in survey research, explains that the very nature of academia makes leaving it difficult. For example, the path from graduate school to a professorship seems clear, but the tight job market means only a few Ph.D.'s will reach that destination, as Simonetta explains:

> Graduate students experience path failure when they assume that the same things that made them successful up to this point will continue to do so when the time finally comes to find an academic position. Discovering that there are no tenure-track job openings in their field or that employers outside academia do not value their academic credentials comes as a painful shock.

Many graduate students fear that searching for a post-academic job is a tacit admission that their years in graduate school have been wasted. As Simonetta describes the phenomenon:

> Almost all of the people in a given Ph.D. program have passed up other opportunities outside of academia. It is transparently clear that their friends and acquaintances who have not made the choice to enter a Ph.D. program are reaping more material and, in many cases, psychological rewards than those who have chosen the Ivory Tower path. It is one thing to have delayed grat-

ification if one ends up in the desired position in academia, but to have to go back out into the same job market that most graduate students shunned five or even ten years ago is likely to be a psychologically wrenching moment.

And, finally, Simonetta notes that the culture of academia reinforces the dynamics described above: "Most academics see themselves as above mere commerce and actively promote themselves as such. A Ph.D. candidate hears this directly and indirectly throughout his or her term as a candidate." Thus, in addition to the generalized peer pressure that stigmatizes those outside the group, academia labels those who attempt to earn a steady living outside the academy as greedy, materialistic sellouts.

Another major concern for graduate students is a fear of losing one's identity. An anthropology graduate student from the University of Michigan, Karen Rignall, describes herself as "terrified and tormented" at the thought of leaving her program:

> I was afraid that I was quitting, that I was weak, that I couldn't finish anything. I loved Morocco and feared that I'd be giving up my relation to the place since I was supposed to do my fieldwork there next year. I was studying for generals at the time, and feared that I was copping out. I'd built my identity around these books I'd read, these people I know, and I thought that no one else would understand me—I'm unique. I worried that I would no longer know what the newest development in theory is, and I wouldn't be able to talk to anyone.

Rignall's fears were not realized. After a year outside academia, "I got over my elitist sensibility and learned that I don't have to talk through theory books to relate to someone," she says. Although she sometimes "feels nostalgic" for the intellectual community of graduate school, she believes that "even older academics can't sustain the intensity that graduate students have."

A former graduate student in philosophy, John DeSanto, worried that he didn't have the skills to get a post-academic job. Combining his story with Rignall's illustrates how graduate school teaches us simultaneously to overestimate and underestimate our abilities. As DeSanto sees it: "You get used to feeling like a nothing in grad school. You don't realize you could do more. A friend who left my department two years before I did tried to tell me that it was okay to leave, but I just didn't hear her." DeSanto left his program to work for Cycorp, a Texas-based artificial intelligence company founded by a former philosophy professor and staffed by dozens of former philosophy grad students. Happy in his new career, he finds that "I talk about philosophy at work these days more than I ever did in grad school."

For others, the decision to leave academia revolves around less dramatic, but no less painful, questions about quality of life. Bryan Garman, a Ph.D. in American studies from Emory, summarizes his dilemma in a single sentence: "Do I want to put my life on hold to make another run at a tenure-track job?" His wife, an attorney, had a good job in Washington, D.C., and after weighing his options, he decided to forgo a nationwide academic job search. Instead, he accepted a teaching job at a prep school so he could live with his wife. In 2005 he became the head of Wilmington Friends School.

Faculty members who decide to leave tenure-track or tenured positions for post-academic careers face a different set of concerns. Alexandra Lord, a British history Ph.D., found a tenure-track job with an ideal two-two teaching load at Montana State University soon after finishing her dissertation. Although she was lucky to find a job in her field, she went on the market again immediately as the isolation of living in Bozeman (made worse by the fact that she did not earn enough to afford a car) caused her to question whether the sacrifices academia required were worth the rewards: "Gradually, I realized that I had given up all of the things which had made me want to be a historian (museums, bookstores, archives, theater, etc.) simply so that I could be a professor teaching kids who were, at best, only marginally interested in British history." Lord quit her job at Montana State and accepted a visiting position at SUNY–New Paltz, thinking she'd be happier on the East Coast. Some questioned her sanity. Why on earth would anyone give up a perfectly good tenure-track job for a nontenured position? Being back on the East Coast did not improve her perspective on the profession, however, and she soon left her job to become a historian for the U.S. Public Health Service. "Academia was not the paradise I dreamed it would be," Lord says. "In academia's defense, however, I will admit that I was extremely naive. No field or profession could have lived up to my idealized vision." She has no regrets about leaving academia but does wish she had faced her ambivalence toward the profession sooner: "I do have a lot of regret (and sometimes anger) about the years I wasted in Bozeman and New Paltz. . . . I should have acknowledged that I didn't like academia earlier, and I should never have listened to people who told me that only losers leave academia."

Whether you are a faculty member or a graduate student, some of your concerns are unique to academia, but others are common to most working adults. Absolutely everyone has to make trade-offs when they accept a job. Maybe the hours are too long, but the pay is good. Maybe the commute is short, but the work is not that interesting. Maybe the work is wonderfully satisfying but pays too little. And once you think you've got it all figured out, you have to do it all over again because your much-beloved boss has been replaced by a hard-headed tyrant and now your dream job is a nightmare. Ultimately, we can't give you any simple answers on how to stay ahead of the shifting sands, because we haven't figured out any of this ourselves (and neither has anyone else). As John Romano told us, academics who ask him for career advice "seem to want answers as institutionalized and direct as academic life. But the world isn't that clear-cut. You must improvise."

Should I Finish My Dissertation?

Among the many fears that can keep a distressed graduate student awake at night, the biggest one is usually: Should I finish my dissertation or not? (And sometimes the question emerges even earlier: Should I quit before even starting my dissertation?) While we can't tell you what the right answer is, we can tell you that you don't have to torture yourself by trying to decide on an absolute "yes" or "no."

Instead, concentrate on taking control of your progress in the short term. This may sound like we're calling for some sort of grad student revolt; we're not. We're just trying to correct the over-inflated idea most grad students have of their adviser's investment in their progress. Admit it: you've probably had nightmares in which your adviser has wreaked Godzilla-like havoc on your tiny studio apartment. As a young civil engineering professor told us: "It was a surprise to me when I became a professor to see how wrong I was about my adviser's level of interest in me. I wish my grad students well, but I don't stay up at night worrying about them or calculating how fast they're working."

Many grad students we interviewed talked about feeling held captive by a slow-moving or indecisive adviser. One humanities student described how his adviser's behavior caused him to leave his program A.B.D. ("all but dissertation" completed). Although the grad student was writing steadily, his adviser took a year to read each chapter he produced and then things got even worse:

> After two years of work on my dissertation in one direction, my advisers pulled the rug out from under me. If graduate school were a company and they were managers, they would've been fired long ago. I was in my seventh year—it was awful. When they told me I was going to have to start over, I thought, "I'm going to have a nervous breakdown and I don't even have health insurance."

Based on his experience, he advises other grad students to beware of "letting sluggish advisers pull you off track." If he did it all over again, he says, "I'd be smarter about it, tougher about it. I'd treat grad school more like a job—work nine to five and meet my adviser with some pages every Friday."

Maybe such time-clock discipline is unrealistic for you. The key here is to unfold that road map for yourself and not let your adviser do all the navigating. Asserting yourself may cause a little friction, but in general your adviser does not have as much interest in you, or power over you, as you imagine.

Whether you are just beginning to question your future as an academic or nearing the end of your proverbial rope, understand that you do have options. Here are some approaches that different alumni have used to get out of their grad school ruts:

Speak frankly with your adviser about your job market concerns, your financial and family pressures, and your personal happiness. Think about how you would like the next few years of your life to look. Is it time to move on? Do you need more financial stability? Is your spouse/partner/parent/favorite pet running out of patience with you? Are you tired of sacrificing the present for an uncertain future? Tell your adviser you'd like to set a schedule for finishing your dissertation by a certain date. While you might think that an adviser would be horrified by such a pragmatic approach, you'll probably be surprised. For example, one professor confided to us that she feels relieved whenever one of her grad students announces that he won't be going on the market for the third or fourth time. "It's a tough market," she acknowledges, "and I'm glad that they have decided to escape the cycle."

Once you've broken the ice with your adviser, you can talk about modifying your project. Writing a shorter, more focused dissertation (as opposed to one that is halfway to becoming an academic publication and primed for the job market) will allow you to earn your degree, but also let you get on with your life. As far as the world outside the academy is concerned, there are two kinds of dissertations: finished and unfinished.

Try taking time off to do something else for six months or a year. If just thinking about your project makes you feel hopeless and miserable, take a break from it to get some perspective. You don't need to decide now if you'll ever finish or not. Take an intensive language course abroad. Do a formal or informal internship (see chapter 3 for more advice). Get out of your head and off your campus, whether by taking a formal leave of absence or a self-imposed sabbatical. You'll earn some money, gain some experience, and maybe even clarify your desire to be an academic. Over and over again, alumni have told us that once the dissertation was no longer the looming presence in their lives, they found it much easier to just write the damn thing. Or they decided that finishing it would just take too much time away from other things they enjoy. It's only a dissertation. If it's haunting you, put a stake through its heart.

Decide that you sure as hell will finish this stupid thing . . . but not right now. Promise yourself that you'll finish your dissertation eventually, and then give yourself permission to pack it up into a box for the present. Rodney Whitlock, a political science Ph.D. who finished his dissertation three years into his new job on Capitol Hill, told us: "I always said that I could finish it in two months, but I just never did it before. At the time I left academia, there were no jobs, so there was no incentive to finish." By stint of sheer will and several trips to Office Depot for legal pads and exactly the right kind of pen, Whitlock got it done in two months, just as he'd predicted. Leaving open the question of when to finish will free you to explore other interests. Come back to your dissertation in a few months, or a few years.

Or you can just let it go. Maybe the topic just doesn't thrill you anymore; maybe the field is getting overcrowded; maybe your project has had so many setbacks it just seems doomed. Make your peace with it. Grad student turned career expert Nick Corcodilos described his reason for leaving Stanford's cognitive psychology program A.B.D. as frustration over a lack of intellectual independence. He wanted to do his own research, not his adviser's, and has no regrets about leaving academia. If you are more ambivalent than Corcodilos, remember that the average person (not to mention most of your relatives) thinks writing a dissertation is odd in the first place. About 99 percent of the population will actually think that you're more sensible and clear-headed for not finishing that 500-page treatise.

Or decide not to decide. There's nothing wrong with hedging your bets. If you're ambivalent about leaving academia, straddle the tracks for a while. Pursue both options simultaneously, and make the big decisions only when forced. The boundary between academia and the post-academic world is more permeable than you may realize.

How to Use Your Grad School Years Wisely

Aside from writing your dissertation and teaching classes, what else are you doing in graduate school? Keep a calendar to measure how you use your time for a week, and see how many hours you spend actually working versus how many hours you spend thinking about working, avoiding working, feeling guilty about not working, pretending to work. . . . You know the game.

You're going to spend at least four or five years in graduate school. The national average is closer to a decade. What will you have to show for yourself besides teaching and research? You need to pursue other interests for a variety of reasons: to make yourself a more interesting person, to keep yourself sane, and to make yourself more marketable to both academic and post-academic employers.

The benefits of testing other interests while you're in grad school are clear when you look at stories of alumni who've tried this approach. Karen Rignall unexpectedly found the confidence to leave the anthropology program at the University of Michigan by working at a part-time job:

> After my first year in grad school, I spent a year in Cairo studying Arabic. I'm half Egyptian and had a strong personal interest in keeping up with the language. When I came back to the U.S., I worked part-time at an Arab community center in Detroit doing fund-raising. My boss was very encouraging and kept saying that he'd hire me in a minute. That enabled me to think that I had some skills, that I could leave academia and someone would hire me.

History Ph.D. Emily Hill discovered that a seemingly irrelevant summer job can carry a lot of weight in a job interview. Her in-

GRAD SCHOOL TIME VS. POST-ACADEMIC TIME

Many of the alumni we interviewed noted that the pace of daily life altered dramatically once they entered the business world. "One day in the business world is equivalent to about three weeks in academia," history Ph.D. turned McKinsey management consultant Emily Hill estimates.

Depending on where you work—and McKinsey is the high-powered corporate extreme—your typical day might change dramatically after you enter the workforce. But those changes are not necessarily for the worse, as Hill describes:

> I used to work all day and accomplish so little—now I get much more done, and without all the procrastination. I go home knowing I've done a good day's work, instead of feeling guilty all the time. I miss drinking coffee in my bathrobe at 11 a.m., but in a way, I also hated myself then for not getting enough done. I worked inefficiently, never felt like I'd accomplished anything. If I go back to academia, and I may someday, I will be ten times more productive than if I had stayed.

Other alumni, such as Rodney Whitlock, a political science Ph.D. who now burns the midnight oil working on Capitol Hill, recalls similar grad school frustrations. "I hated the feeling that you were never really busy, and never really not busy. I hated the nagging feeling over the weekends," Whitlock remembers.

The faster pace of post-academic jobs means that the standard for quality work is quite different as well. Steve Sampson, doctoral student and writer for a tech company, learned in his first months on the job that "the goal is not so much to get things 'right' as it is to get things done 'as well as possible' in a brief amount of time."

terviewers at McKinsey, a consulting firm, questioned her ability to work as part of a team because she had been doing solitary academic work for so long. Hill won them over by describing her summer job leading backpacking trips for teenagers. McKinsey's concerns are shared by many employers. It's good advice for any academic to round out his or her experience with group activities, anything from building houses with Habitat for Humanity to organizing a department softball team.

Sometimes the connection between outside activities and post-academic careers is just plain obvious. While earning his American studies Ph.D., Bryan Garman spent several summers teaching gifted middle school students. That experience helped him figure out whether or not he'd enjoy teaching students younger than college age. It also gave him crucial experience and recommendations when he eventually applied for a high school teaching job.

Even within your academic program, a little diversification can go a long way. John Rumm, a University of Delaware Ph.D. who now works for the research firm History Associates, credits his broad interest in the history of business (rather than a smaller subfield of history) with making his skills more relevant to post-academic employers. Try mixing a little Spanish with your political science, or a little anthropology with your art history. Your academic work will be strengthened, and your post-academic options will expand.

Scientists should "spend time developing skills (leadership, communication, organizational, etc.) outside of the lab (and document them!) so that you can show prospective employers that you are not 'just another disgruntled postdoc looking for a way out,'" advises Sharyl Nass, Ph.D., of the Institute of Medicine. "Show them that you have other interests and abilities beyond the lab."

Whatever your interests, you can get started broadening your experience right now. You're already surrounded by a wealth of resources—your campus is a mini-universe of possibilities. Take advantage of your university:

- Audit classes in the law school, the business school, the medical school, or any department that interests you. If your university doesn't offer what you're looking for, try another campus.

- Get to know the staff at the computer center and take a class in website design or network technology. You have access to an amazing amount of technology and know-how for free; take advantage of it while you can.
- Earn some extra cash through a part-time job unrelated to your academic interests. Try the greenhouse, the rare books room, the admissions office, the computer center, or the art museum.
- Use your skills in a different context. Design posters for the campus theater company, build a web page for a campus group, write for a university publication, or do fund-raising.
- Volunteer your time to improve town-gown relations. Start a tutoring program or story hour for local kids. Get involved in local or national politics or causes.

All of these experiences can add up to important skills and knowledge if you decide later that you want to pursue a career outside the academy. And if you're happy and successful inside academia, then you've strengthened your candidacy for an assistant professorship as well.

Whodunit? And How Can I Do It Too?

If you decide to change careers, you will probably have to pay your dues (at least for a little while) in the form of low pay and little prestige. How do academics handle this transition? Let's take a closer look at one Ph.D.'s progress from office secretary to full-fledged, card-carrying private eye.

While Michelle Squiteri was trying to finish her dissertation on medieval and Renaissance love lyrics at the University of California, Berkeley, she took a job as a secretary at a private investigation firm to earn extra money. "Maybe I had an eye out, knowing that I needed an alternative to academia," she said. "The investigators were doing research in public records, interviewing people, and writing reports—it seemed similar to what I was doing." While it was "painful to realize I had to go back to square one," Squiteri calls her secretarial job "one of the best things I did."

For a year and a half, she worked at the PI firm while producing chapters of her dissertation more quickly and steadily than she had in years: "When I got into work that was professional and interesting, I just felt better about myself. I knew that I could finish my dissertation then. I set a deadline and kept it." The perspective she gained from working outside academia made the dissertation seem like a manageable task, rather than the end-all, be-all of her existence.

The other important benefit of her job was that it opened her eyes to another possible career: "When I saw what the investigators did, I knew that I liked it, and I knew that I could do it." After learning the ropes as a secretary, Squiteri sought advice on how to make the leap to investigator. She arranged an information interview (more on these important strategies in chapter 3) with a well-known criminal investigator. During the interview, Squiteri explained what she'd learned in the PI office and why her academic skills would be useful in investigative work: "I told him that sonnets are full of deliberate vagueness and hinting: readers have to unravel the mystery, find the clues. In *The Hound of the Baskervilles,* Sherlock Holmes tucks a volume of Petrach's poetry in his pocket on his way to work on a case. It's perfect!" Her contact suggested she start by looking for a job in civil investigation, such as insurance fraud work, to learn the skills of the trade, and then move up into criminal work. She followed his advice and now works as a full-time criminal investigator in a job that she enjoys enormously, but that also leaves her "energy and time for myself."

While working as an investigator, Squiteri gave the academic market one more try: "Already having a job as an investigator made the academic job market less stressful. I felt much more secure and much less desperate. My husband decided he was going to teach no matter what the price, but I felt insecure and horrified by the idea of having a degree and being on my own as a teacher." In the end, she was offered a tenure-track job at a Midwestern university, but she turned it down. Knowing that

THE HIDDEN VALUE OF MENIAL OFFICE WORK

No one with an advanced degree should waste his or her time in a low-level office job, right? Well, even in the most Ph.D.-friendly workplaces, employers still want to see evidence that you've got some basic office skills, warns John Rumm, a Ph.D. who works for History Associates in Rockville, Maryland.

"If we're looking at two résumés from graduate students, and one has worked at an office job and one has never set foot outside academia, we're going to take the one who's worked in an office before. It doesn't matter if it's a low-level job or unrelated to your interest," Rumm says.

Why is office experience so important? Because it shows that you can work with other people in addition to performing certain basic tasks, like making a business phone call, sending a fax, or writing a memo, Rumm explains. "That way, we know the person we hire won't be walking around the office starry-eyed."

So should you run out and join the secretarial pool? No. But you're bound to have done some office work along the way in a part-time job or as a volunteer. Without even realizing it, you've gained experience that you can use to convince an employer that you're right for the job.

she already had a lucrative, satisfying job that would allow her to stay in the Bay Area she loved made the choice much easier.

She has not abandoned all things academic, however. Squiteri recently spent six months teaching in France and published an article in a French academic journal. She would like to publish her dissertation eventually and plans to return to France to teach every few years. The flexibility of investigative work allows her to pursue her intellectual interests without having to compromise her quality of life.

So What Am *I* Going to Do?

While it looks like Squiteri hedged her bets expertly and even managed to pull down an academic job offer in a tough job market, she freely admits that she had no grand master plan for her life. Most people's careers have some logical continuity to them in retrospect, but it's rare to find someone who claims to have known in advance what they would love or hate about Job A, and how that experience would prompt them toward Job B and then Job C. We found that in interviewing the enormous range of people for this book, the number one answer to the question "How did you get where you are today?" was "Serendipity."

So what good does that do you? Well, it takes the pressure off. You're not psychic; you can't possibly predict all the moves ahead. Be open to unexpected possibilities and follow your instincts. If a job or volunteer project or hobby makes you enormously happy, run with it. A career will likely develop out of it in one way or another. And if it doesn't, you'll never regret spending time on something you love. E. L. Doctorow has a great quote about writing that we think also applies to divining a career path: "It's like driving at night. Your headlights only light up the road 30 feet in front you, but that's enough to get you all the way home."

The biggest difference between academic careers and post-academic careers is that the road is almost too well-lit in academia—you don't even need your headlights. The path is excruciatingly clear for humanists and social scientists. You look for a job at the same time everyone else does, and if you don't find work, you simply wait until next year to repeat the process. The free-form post-academic job market can look downright scary to someone coming from the well-ordered academic universe. Of course, if you're a scientist, you may face the opposite problem. You're at the mercy of your advisers. As Rob Peters, a Ph.D. in biology and author of *Getting What You Came For: The Smart Student's Guide to Earning a Master's or Ph.D.* (Farrar, Straus and Giroux, 1997), puts it, "After all those years in graduate school, I still couldn't figure out where the jobs were!" Scientists used to tangling with such mysterious forces may become resigned to passivity, so you, too, will have to reinvent your approach to job hunting for the post-academic world.

Six Myths about Post-Academic Careers

In order to see through the fog that sometimes surrounds us in grad school, you first have to abandon some myths about post-academic careers and replace them with questions that will help you think about your skills and your potential in a more positive and productive way.

1. No one would hire me. I have no useful skills.

Academics do suffer the disadvantage of being misunderstood by most employers. Few people will recognize at a glance that your research and teaching skills can be an asset to their company. You must figure out how your experience can benefit them—the burden is on you. Try the exercises in the next chapter to help you recognize the many talents you've developed as a teacher and researcher. Also, remember that when we ask how someone's new career is similar to his or her former academic life, nine out of ten times the answer is "I do a lot of teaching in my work." Figure out what the analogies are in your line of work, and then you can persuade others.

2. Your dissertation is your most valuable asset.

While it's true that you have many valuable skills, the specific content of your dissertation is of little interest or value to most people outside academia. If you begin your job search with the idea that you are an expert on a particular topic seeking a place to ply your trade, you are likely to fail. What is valuable about your dissertation is what you learned in the process of writing it, not the product itself. Ann Kirschner, an English Ph.D. and president of the consulting firm Comma International, emphasizes the value of analytical skills in today's economy: "There is simply nothing better than the liberal arts to prepare brains to accommodate the pace of today's world, where knowledge changes so quickly that you can't master any field, but can only gain the fundamentals and the ability to acquire the rest."

3. People who work in the business world are stupid and boring

If all of your friends and associates are academics, you may think this statement is true. Graduate school does forge wonderful, lasting friendships, but it also cocoons you with people who are exactly like you. Academia has its share of dull or boring folks, as does every other field. But the post-academic world offers a greater variety of backgrounds and more room for interaction than academia.

"The biggest myth that academics have about the world of business and government is that they'll be working with people who are intellectually inferior," says Howard Scheiber, a Ph.D. in linguistics who now works as director of staff development for the New York Public Library. "This just isn't the case: there are very bright people out there, as smart as any you'll find on campus."

4. Jobs in the business world are stupid and boring.

Remember how when you were fifteen everything was boring? Shakespeare was boring, quantum physics was boring, the Grand Canyon was boring. . . . Pretty much everything was officially too dull for words. Why? Because you didn't know enough to appreciate it. But that's why you're in grad school. You got hooked once you realized that the more you learned about a topic, the more interesting it was. Treat your career exploration as another research project. Don't assume surface appearances are correct. Academic life is one of about ten million possible careers. How can you be sure that the each of the other 99.9 percent of jobs in the universe isn't for you?

5. It's too late to change careers.

In a world where layoffs and takeovers are commonplace, the job market is full of people scrambling to update their résumés, leap into different fields, or start over in midcareer. A 2002 Department of Labor survey reported that workers had an average of ten different jobs before they were forty, so there's no shame in changing tacks. The key to successful career changing is learning the customs and vocabulary of the field you want to enter and then articulating your value. "People just don't do jobs forever anymore," insists Carol Barash, a former professor who now runs her own advertising agency. "The tenure-track model of having the same job for life is outdated."

6. I'm too old.

Oh no you're not. After we gave a talk at the Modern Language Association convention in 1998, someone came up to us and said, "That's fine for you—but I'm much older than you are, and things are different for me." As it turned out, she was younger than we were. In fact, faculty members and older graduate students have a greater wealth of experience and contacts to draw upon than someone who's only a few years out of college. Remember, we're not advocating making sudden, radical changes in your life. Gaining new experience, investigating other uses for your skills, and keeping a foot in another career is all wise advice at any age. Also, graduate students and professors are paid modestly compared to most other careers. That means employers can afford to hire you.

Five Questions for Rethinking Graduate School

As you read the following chapters, try to replace the myths with these questions. Focus on figuring out what you want for yourself, and don't worry about what you should or shouldn't be doing:

1. How much experience have you had in the world outside academia?

How many people do you know who aren't academics? What do you enjoy doing aside from your intellectual work? Did you have another job before coming to graduate school? How do your peers talk about people who have other kinds of jobs?

2. What do you think it would be like outside academia?

Have you ever worked nine to five? What would you miss about academic life? Think of your friends who aren't academics.

"I GOT MY FIRST FULL-TIME JOB AT FIFTY"

Barbara Fisher finished her Ph.D. at Columbia in 1976. She taught part-time at several New York colleges for the next twenty-five years while raising two children. She also wrote book reviews on the side and had a regular column in the *Boston Globe*. At the age of fifty, she decided she was ready for a change.

Fisher started by thinking about "what world I wanted to work in" and decided that a fine art auction house would be a glamorous and exciting environment. She networked her way into a job at Christie's, where she writes marketing proposals designed to persuade owners of large collections to sell their items through Christie's.

"It's absolutely inspirational to get your first full-time job at the age of fifty," she says. She credits her experience writing book reviews on deadline with persuading Christie's to hire her.

AGING LIKE FINE WINE

Another alum who changed careers late in life took a more gradual approach. Organic chemistry professor Lanny Repogle slowly developed his wine-making skills during the thirty-one years he taught at San Jose State University. He took early retirement in order to devote himself to making wine full-time. He and his wife produced 7,500 cases of wine in 2005 under their Fenestra Winery label.

Does his organic chemistry Ph.D. help him in his new career? "If there's a problem with the wine, I'm better equipped than the average person to figure out what went wrong," Repogle says. And he also uses his teaching skills when he holds wine tastings for the public. But the best part of wine making, he says, is "the creative effort, seeing how wines develop and change over time, and the pride of making a wine that people enjoy."

Who loves their work the most? Whose work interests you the most? Which aspects appeal to you? What does that tell you about yourself? (If no other job besides a professorship appeals to you even in the abstract, then maybe you don't know much about what else is out there.)

3. Are you happy in graduate school?

Sure, "depressed graduate student" is redundant, but honestly. . . . Would you like to make a change but feel you can't, or don't know how? A short vacation from academia, in the form of a part-time job or volunteer project in a completely different field, could help you rediscover what you love about academia or show you alternatives that you would enjoy more.

4. What are your pressing concerns? Family? Finances?

Maybe you're pretty sure that you want to be an academic but recognize that your dream may not come true. You may have a spouse and children; you may be racking up enormous amounts of debt; you may be taxing the patience of your parents or whoever is helping you pay for school. Maybe your significant other is also an academic and you can't find jobs at the same institution. Keeping one foot outside academia, in a part-time job or a computer class, may help you adjust more quickly, in both practical and emotional terms, if it turns out that you have to leave academia.

5. Why did you come to grad school in the first place?

Is your motivation for staying the same? Life as a professor probably looks pretty different to you now, compared to when you first mailed off that grad school application. How do your expectations match up to reality?

Anna Patchias, a University of Virginia English Ph.D. who worked part-time as a tutor during grad school and now runs her own tutoring company, recommends asking yourself these kinds of questions repeatedly throughout your grad school years:

> I think people need to be much more aware of the sacrifices required for a Ph.D. in the humanities before they take the leap. You should ask yourself: "How am I growing toward or away from the profession? What is the state of the market in my field?

What would my salary be? How much debt will I have? How long will it take to pay if off?"

Asking yourself these "cold-blooded questions" early on, Patchias suggests, can help you maintain a realistic picture of what lies ahead and what the trade-offs may be.

Your Eclectic Mix

We've tried to show you throughout this chapter that there isn't a single correct path that leads to post-academic bliss. Everyone's story is different, and you'll have to make your own decisions. But one element that ties together all of the options that we've presented here is what one of our interviewees calls your "eclectic mix." In other words, everyone has to discover which features of academia are most important to them, and then find some combination of activities that fulfills those needs. Your job doesn't have to be your only intellectual stimulation. In fact, some people we interviewed think of themselves as having never left academia, even though they have post-academic jobs. They simply choose to pursue only the elements of academic life that appeal to them.

Two alumni stories in particular, one from a chief executive officer of a major corporation and one from a woman who cleans houses for a living, reminded us how varied different people's eclectic mixes can be. When Robert Brawer was downsized from his job as an English professor at the University of Wisconsin–Madison in 1975, he never imagined that he'd become CEO of Maidenform, Inc. His wife's family owned the company and helped him get a start in the marketing department, but adjusting to the business world wasn't easy for him. Brawer worked his way up and learned all sides of the business, from fashion to manufacturing to finance. He's proud of having used his writing skills to improve the firm's marketing research strategy and spent a total of twenty years at Maidenform, serving as CEO from 1990 to 1995.

But Brawer remained a teacher at heart. He missed being in

the classroom, so he also taught adult "great books" classes at the local library during the years he worked at Maidenform. Although his business success might seem like enough to make anyone's life complete, he recognized and addressed an unfilled need through his eclectic mix.

Louise Rafkin's search for an eclectic mix began after she left the creative writing program at the University of California, Santa Cruz. She decided that although she loved writing, "teaching American literature and composition to a gaggle of undergraduates was stressful and not very gratifying." To support herself as a writer, she began cleaning houses. She has sincere enthusiasm for a good vacuum cleaner and likes setting her own hours, but writing remains her passion. Her work has been published in the *New York Times,* the *Los Angeles Times*, and in her collection of essays, *Other People's Dirt: A Housecleaner's Curious Adventures.*

Brawer and Rafkin followed their instincts, and each ended up successful and satisfied, in entirely unexpected ways. For them, the complementary part of the equation was easy to identify. But for other people, the right ingredients for their eclectic mix are more elusive, as the following story shows. Sabrina Wenrick left an adjunct teaching position in California for a medical writing job in Washington, D.C. After she'd been in the business world for about four months, we asked her what she thought about her experience. Her answer shows that the formation of her eclectic mix will be guided by a different set of values:

> When I was teaching, I used to feel that my job was my service, my way of doing good in the world. Now I work in an office and I like what I do, but it's over at 5 p.m. and my weekends are free. So now what I need to do is decide how I want to do my service, how I want to do good in the world. And it's kind of liberating, that I can choose to do anything, that it doesn't need to be the same as what I do to earn a living.

What we love about Wenrick is the energy and creativity with which she pursues her personal eclectic mix. We hope to inspire the same kind of enthusiasm for self-discovery in you. We can't give you a road map to your post-academic career, but if you're willing to risk the first few steps, you'll discover that you already know how to find your own way.

....

POST-ACADEMIC PROFILE:
TOM MAGLIOZZI, COHOST OF NPR'S *CAR TALK*,
PH.D. IN CHEMICAL ENGINEERING

Before finding fame and fortune as cohost of *Car Talk,* the most popular show on National Public Radio, Tom Magliozzi was a chemical engineering professor. He earned his Ph.D. while working as a mechanic in the garage he owned with his brother Ray. He found a full-time teaching job, "and it was good for about five years," he says. "But suddenly . . . it was over. I reached (through deep thought, meditation, and prayer) a miraculous epiphany: Teaching sucks."

According to Magliozzi's "New Theory of Learning," there are three major problems with the way schools and universities try to educate students:

- First, students must learn by doing rather than listening. "Don't let an 'expert' stand in front of people and tell them everything he knows. . . . The overhead projector has done more to destroy learning than any other thing I can think of."
- Second, hypothetical examples are poor substitutes for reality. Students need to experience business, medicine, engineering, and so on firsthand in order to gain the knowledge they'll need in the real world.
- Finally, learning should be about solving problems that are important to the students. If a teacher allows his students to "learn backward," meaning that students set out to fix a problem and then acquire necessary skills and information along the way, they will never lack for motivation.

And although Magliozzi says he has quit teaching, anyone who listens to *Car Talk* knows that the show is the perfect example of his New Theory of Learning in action.

2 How Do I Figure Out What Else to Do?

Soul-Searching Before Job Searching

If you've been thinking about exploring post-academic careers, you may already have consulted some career books. Maybe you've even taken career assessments (like the Myers-Briggs Type Indicator or the Jackson Vocational Interest Survey) to figure out what jobs best suit you. Maybe you've found these exercises helpful. Or maybe you're more like Kelly Flynn, a frustrated graduate student in English who plowed through some classic career manuals only to conclude, "I don't know what color my parachute is. I think it's plaid."

Or you might be one of those people who always skips this kind of "get in touch with yourself" chapter in career books. Either you're not interested in answering a bunch of silly questions or you're already pretty sure what field you want to enter. Fair enough. You can skip ahead to chapter 3 and we won't be hurt.

But we encourage you to give our version of the "how to find yourself" chapter a quick look before you go. In addition to career exercises designed specifically for academics, this chapter also includes a special collection of a few dozen alumni profiles grouped by field (consulting, teaching, government) to help you narrow down your choices. We can't promise that we will identify your parachute color, but we think our alumni stories will at least spark your imagination.

You won't find any easy answers in this chapter. Unfortu-

CAREER GUIDE SUGGESTIONS

Your favorite bookstore is overflowing with career guides, but few of them address the needs of former academics. Here's a list of the books that we found most helpful (for updated listings, be sure to visit our website at www.careersforphds.com for updated links):

- *What Color Is Your Parachute?*, by Richard Nelson Bolles (Ten Speed Press, 2006)
- *Through the Brick Wall: How to Job-Hunt in a Tight Market*, by Kate Wendleton (Random House, 1992)
- *Creating a Life Worth Living: A Practical Course in Career Design for Artists, Innovators, and Others Aspiring to a Creative Life*, by Carol Lloyd (HarperCollins, 1997)
- *Zen and the Art of Making a Living: A Practical Guide to Creative Career Design*, by Laurence G. Boldt (Penguin, 1999)
- *Hi-Tech Careers for Low-Tech People*, by William A. Schaffer (Ten Speed Press, 1999)
- *Alternative Careers in Science: Leaving the Ivory Tower*, 2nd ed., edited by Cynthia Robbins-Roth (Academic Press, 2005)
- *I Could Do Anything If I Only Knew What It Was: How to Discover What You Really Want and How to Get It*, by Barbara Sher (Dell, 1995)

We also both found Margaret Newhouse's *Outside the Ivory Tower* enormously helpful and inspiring, but this book can be difficult to find. Try ordering it directly from Harvard University Career Services, or ask for it at your university's career office.

nately, there's no such thing when it comes to a career search. Don't let this revelation fill you with dread. In fact, embrace the ambiguity. If that task sounds daunting, just remember that none of the questions you answered in graduate school had easy answers either, so you should be right at home. Your thesis or dissertation probably posed a question so difficult that it has taken you several years to answer, right? Well, the good news is that career searches tend to go faster than dissertations.

There's no such thing as a one-size-fits-all career exploration exercise, so we've tried to design questions geared toward academics and follow up with examples of how these principles applied to other alumni. For now, we're going to ask you to take a radical step away from your piles of library books or your laboratory rats. Devote a few hours to yourself. It's alarming to realize that many graduate students have spent more hours thinking about a conference paper than exploring their own lives. Academics are not encouraged to think about whether or not they enjoy what they do. Admitting that you like teaching better than research, or vice versa, is not wise except on certain campuses where one of the two is clearly preferred. We're asking you to think about something more subtle than whether or not you want to work in academia. We're asking you to think about which aspects of academic life and work bring you pleasure and which parts make you miserable. Once you have that knowledge, you can not only make better decisions about what kind of academic life might suit you (a teaching-focused job with lots of committee work versus a laboratory-centered job that requires little to no student contact) but also about whether you may be happier in another profession altogether.

The following exercises are designed to help you identify your strengths and clarify your interests so that you can find the right career for you.

Take Inventory

We're big believers in pro and con lists. It sounds simple, but you may be surprised by what you find. Make a two-column list of everything you love and everything you hate about academia so you can view your experience more objectively.

Here's what Maggie's pro and con list looks like:

Hates	Loves
Solitude	Flexibility
Tight job market	Intellectual engagement
Humorless academic writing	Working with language
Speaking/writing to a very small audience	Sharing a love of books with colleagues

The tenure system   Mentoring students
Geographic limitations   Working in archives

And here's Sue's pro and con list:

Hates	Loves
Planning classes, grading papers	Mentoring students
Narrow, abstract research	Exploring new fields of interest
Geographic limitations	Campus life
Academic writing	Public speaking
Sitting through long seminars	Independent work
Rigid hierarchy, poor management	Funny, interesting colleagues

These are the same lists that were included in the first edition of this book, when Maggie and I both had different jobs than we have now. What's interesting is that—without being conscious of it—we have both moved on to jobs that fit our list of "loves" more closely and that suit us much better.

The point of making a chart like this is to show that everyone experiences academia differently. Just as our lists of pros and cons differ—and we were in the same department at the same time—yours will be different from those around you. Unfortunately, most of us spend our grad school years trying to mold ourselves into the perfect job candidate and end up squashing some of those personal instincts. The point of this chapter is to remind yourself what you enjoy and what you do well, without censoring yourself.

So where do you go from here? You can let yourself be guided by one of the items on your pro list, like Robin Wagner, a medieval Chinese history Ph.D., did. She knew that she loved to teach but didn't enjoy the solitary research that academia required. She first applied for a management consulting job with Booz Allen Hamilton, only to find that the position required stronger quantitative skills than she had to offer. She persuaded the firm that her teaching abilities made her a perfect fit for another job—as a trainer of consultants—and was quickly hired. Wagner was able to use the skills she enjoyed most to gain significant business experience and travel around the world.

On the other hand, you may find direction by focusing on what you don't like about university life. For example, the geographical restrictions of academic job hunting had always topped Mark Johnson's con list. After he finished up his coursework for a Ph.D. in English at Boston University, he decided to return to his native San Diego. "The call of surfing was stronger than that of teaching anywhere at any price," he recalls. "As for a job, I reckoned I'd make one happen."

While surfing, doing freelance writing jobs, and finishing his dissertation, Johnson answered a classified ad for a technical writer at Intuit. He wasn't entirely sure what technical writing was, but he had used Intuit's Quicken software to track his (meager) finances. Between his freelance articles and his demonstrated knowledge of Intuit's products, Johnson got the job and was able to stay in the city he loved.

What if your pros and cons are more muddled than Wagner's and Johnson's? Try asking your friends and family what they've observed about you. When are you happiest? What frustrates you? Shannon Zimmerman, a University of Georgia English Ph.D., told us that his wife "saw what I could do when I felt very limited." She had noticed that he always started off the semester excited about teaching, but became gloomy and miserable by the end. She pointed out that he was skilled at making web pages and discussion lists for his classes and that he had always enjoyed doing journalism on the side. Couldn't those interests add up to another career? Zimmerman drew up a résumé highlighting the skills that his wife described and landed a job as a project manager with the Motley Fool personal finance website. A few years later, Zimmerman moved on to Morningstar, where he's able to use his writing skills more fully as a mutual fund analyst.

Even if you're lucky enough to have a perceptive and compassionate spouse, leaving academia can be incredibly painful.

SHOULD I BE AN ENTREPRENEUR?

Being independent thinkers, many graduate alumni are attracted to the idea of starting their own businesses. After years of being shackled by geographic restrictions and the academic calendar, the idea of working where you want when you want may sound appealing. Indeed, a surprising number of the alumni we interviewed have found satisfying careers as freelance journalists, proposal writers for nonprofits, and small business owners.

For Annie Hurlbut, an A.B.D. in anthropology, the process began when she was doing fieldwork in Peru. She sent her mother a beautiful hand-knit sweater as a birthday present; that gift sparked a mother-daughter business partnership that has grown into a successful mail-order clothing company called Peruvian Connection. Hurlbut left her grad program without completing her degree, but she runs her business with an eye toward helping the Peruvian women who knit for her by paying them extremely well and by founding two day-care centers for their children.

Patrick Byrne, the CEO of Overstock.com and a Ph.D. in philosophy from Stanford, explains the academic-entrepreneurial connection this way: "Being a graduate student prepared me emotionally to become an entrepreneur. Graduate school makes you comfortable with psychic stress. It makes you comfortable sticking to your guns when you're in a room where everyone thinks your ideas are wrong."

But think carefully before you decide to head out on your own. Several alumni reminded us that surviving graduate school doesn't automatically equip you to survive the business world. Being self-employed brings freedom but also burdens—like irregular paychecks. If you're already in debt from graduate school, starting your own business might not be the best first step. Paula Foster Chambers, a Ph.D. in rhetoric and composition from Ohio State, decided to parlay her years of writing-instruction experience into a career as a freelance communications consultant. "I slaved away in my home office trying to start a consulting practice with no business experience whatsoever," she recalls. "In many respects I actually did pretty well, but getting clients to hire me was not one of them, and that of course is the one thing that matters most in business: do you have any actual customers?" Now happily employed as the director of development for the Los Angeles Children's Chorus, Chambers explains, "I should have gotten a job in the business world before trying to start my own business. That would have helped me understand the business mind-set, which in turn would have helped me sell myself effectively when starting my business."

Many scholars are reluctant to give up the most fulfilling parts of teaching and research, or the flexibility that goes with these activities. After having spent years in academia, you may find it hard to let go.

If you're grieving about giving up the things on your pro list, don't despair. This is really a lost-and-found exercise. You may not be able to see it from here, but over and over again alumni tell us that the intellectual stimulation or the teaching challenges that they loved in academia are big parts of their new post-academic careers as well. For example, an enormous variety of Ph.D.'s tell us their new careers—as policy wonks, management consultants, public relations executives, and computer gurus—involve some form of teaching. Just because you're not turning in grades at the end of the semester doesn't mean that you're not using your ability to mentor, instruct, and inspire.

And you may find, as Shannon Zimmerman did, that your fear of intellectual stagnation is unfounded. "I was afraid that I was leaving the world of ideas," he said, "but instead I find that I've actually entered the world of ideas."

Break It Down

This exercise can also help you avoid the common mistake of thinking that your extensive knowledge of a certain subject area is your most valuable asset. As many of the examples in this book demonstrate, the thread that leads most former academics to their post-academic jobs is not subject matter but a skill set. Wagner didn't have to work in Chinese history to be happy; she just had to teach. Zimmerman didn't have to continue focusing on Marxist readings of the Romantic poets in order to be happy; he just needed to continue exploring the world of ideas.

Even if you can identify your pros and cons, you will probably need to be more specific than "I like teaching" or "I like researching" in order to apply that knowledge to post-academic career hunting. What exactly do you like about teaching? Is it working with students? Or public speaking? Or designing lesson plans? Breaking down your love of teaching into smaller parts can help you better understand yourself and also help you make a stronger case to an employer.

- First, think about the process of pursuing your scholarly interests, not the content of your work. List all the activities you've done: teaching, research, staff training, administration of a group or laboratory, community service, committee work, political activism, participating in professional conferences.
- Narrow down your list to the three or four activities that meant the most to you. List the tasks associated with each activity.
- Finally, write down the skills associated with each task.

Here are a few examples:

Activity: Being a teaching assistant for an upper-level art history class.

Tasks: Preparing short-term and long-term lesson plans, leading discussions, gathering and organizing slides, lecturing occasionally, grading papers, settling grade disputes, meeting with students before and after papers were due, mentoring students, evaluating students, working with administrators on behalf of students, writing letters of recommendation.

Skills: Organizational ability, planning and scheduling, public speaking, ability to translate complex concepts to new learners, diplomacy, interpersonal skills, supervisory skills, risk taking, interviewing.

Activity: Running lab experiments on mouse genetics.

Tasks: Supervising undergraduate lab assistants, designing experiments, caring for mice, keeping accurate daily records, analyzing results, performing quantitative and statistical analysis, operating laboratory equipment, writing up results, reporting to adviser, applying for grants.

Skills: Management skills, long-term planning, attention to detail, computer modeling, project management, complex problem solving, analytical skills.

SHOULD I TEACH HIGH SCHOOL?

Harrison Scott Key, a theater Ph.D. from Southern Illinois University–Carbondale, left his job at Mississippi State University and, after a brief detour through university fund-raising, finds himself happily teaching rhetoric and literature at Chamberlain-Hunt Academy, a Christian boarding school in Mississippi. He offers advice to those considering secondary school teaching careers.

Why did you leave academia?

I just didn't want to do it anymore. My kind of teaching and writing—like most teachers—took so much heart and so much guts that you have to love it passionately to be able to do it. And I didn't love it anymore. I wanted to hang out with my wife. The hardest part was realizing that—after all that effort and all that study and nearly a decade of planning and dreaming and thinking and writing—I just wanted a change. It wasn't some external force: it was me. I just didn't like it anymore.

How did you end up in your job at the boarding school?

I had spent the previous four years teaching at a summer program for honors high school students, and that was great fun. I knew secondary teaching would be fun, that I liked high school kids as much as (if not more than) college students. High school kids are far more impressed and impressionable: two qualities any teacher should love. And in truth, I generally find my high school students to be as wily and perceptive as college kids. And they're less occupied with sex and drugs and music and discovering themselves than college kids are (at least at my school).

So how does a man teach high school and still have a family and a wife and kids and not live in a cardboard box? The only answer for me was to teach at a boarding school, where housing (and sometimes food) is usually provided. So I looked at boarding schools, and I had an old college friend who was the principal at a boarding school, and the rest is easy to figure out.

What do you like most about teaching at this level?

One nice thing about a boarding school is that it's so similar to a college: there's a level of collegiality and fraternity. You're always around each other. You play together, work together. Very home-away-from-home. You can talk about the lesson as you walk to lunch; you can show up at dinner and tell all your cadets about an assignment you forgot to give; you can help them study on the weekends; you can really be a teacher.

Also, teachers at boarding schools can often write their own curricula, use their own books (or no books). Teachers are treated like professionals. I've even been given release time to write and publish, and guess what—I can write whatever I want. Since coming here in August, I've published in the *Chronicle of Higher Education* and have begun freelancing with *World Magazine.*

How is teaching secondary school similar to college-level teaching?

I teach mostly juniors and seniors, and these kids are so close in age to college freshmen that it's not much of a change. The only real difference is that these younger kids have fewer facts in their heads, but they still feel the same emotions, ask the same questions, have the same fears, hold the same curiosities. They're no different than college students, and in a way they are easier to teach: the students here crave models, leaders, mentors. This is a great change from disinterested or too-cool-for-school students in college.

How does teaching secondary school differ from college-level teaching?

Lots of people probably think it's intellectually inferior to teach high school, but it's not. All teaching is really a matter of problem solving: how do I connect *this* idea, *this* technique with *that* human being? How do I get them to *know* it and not just know *about* it? This is true whether you're teaching junior high, high school, college. Teaching will always be an intellectual feat—tiring, frustrating, impossible, rewarding, all of it.

It's sometimes hard when you find yourself trying to teach something so pedestrian: like why reading is good, why taking notes is hard, what "education" means. This is common with younger kids. But it was really the same way in college. In most colleges and universities, you'll find yourself explaining the same kinds of things. So that's not a real drawback here.

What kind of person would fit well into secondary school teaching? What kind of person would likely be miserable there?

As with any teacher in any school, you have to love the subject and know it like nobody's business. You must have energy, so much energy, and joy, lots of joy. Kids need joy. But you also must not fear discipline. Secondary school kids need it badly. Softies from higher ed—especially the pacifist kind who believe that discipline equals meanness—need to stay in college. These softies don't realize that kids crave, absolutely crave, a standard and a model. If you can't give them a standard, hold them to it, and model right behavior, then you belong elsewhere.

What skills are important in secondary school teaching?

You need to be better at listening. College teaching is all about the master lecturer or genius seminar professor. Listening only happens at the seminar table, if there. In high school, especially a boarding school, you have to have real relationships.

You also have to like kids: hanging out with them, talking to them, listening, playing Frisbee, driving them to the airport, explaining the world to them, and hearing how they see it. You have to be ready to live and eat and sleep and breathe your job. I work quite a few twelve-hour days: teaching, preparing, writing, just hanging out with the kids.

What are some misconceptions about secondary school teaching?

A lot of folks might look down on high school teaching because it's so often badly done in our country, but that doesn't mean you shouldn't do it. It's a vicious cycle: secondary teaching is less prestigious, so better teachers go elsewhere, which makes it even less prestigious, and then you end up with the kind of secondary education we have in this country. We need good teachers here probably more than anywhere else except in elementary school, including the college level.

A lot of graduate students and unhappy new Ph.D.'s probably see secondary teaching as failure. You can't hack it on the college level, that kind of thing. But if you believe in the concept of a calling—and I do—then it's simply a matter of "Are you called to teach high school?" If you are and you have a master's or Ph.D., all the better. At good private and boarding schools, you find a whole lot of doctors and masters. That should inspire confidence. We don't come to secondary teaching because we've failed at college teaching. We come because we like high school students, because we like the boarding climate, because we like teaching here and not there, and most of all—for me—because I wanted to teach and write and publish in a broader field. I'm not worried about tenure and making some giant splash in some tiny field: I write what I want to write—essays, stories, articles, whatever.

How do you see your teaching career changing over time?

I like organizing things, fixing things, building consensus, so I could see myself in administration one day. The perfect job would be to teach one or two classes and do administrative work, like being a faculty dean at a good private school. I've also considered a full-time career in journalism. But I'll probably always teach somewhere. I'm a teacher; it's what I do.

Looking Backward: Seven Stories

Now it's time to expand your personal inventory to include life beyond the university. Everything counts here: childhood triumphs, high school activities, half-forgotten hobbies. In this exercise, you'll look back at the whole of your life, not just your work experience, to find out what makes you happy and how you can be successful.

We've borrowed the Seven Stories approach from Kate Wendleton's *Through the Brick Wall: How to Job-Hunt in a Tight Market*—a great resource for career-changers like us. Here's how you start: Write down twenty enjoyable accomplishments from any time in your life. Include anything you enjoyed doing that you also did well. You can mix childhood memories with recent events, and big professional moments with trivial victories. Anything goes. It may take you a day or two to come up with your list of twenty. Then pick out the seven stories that speak to you most strongly: the ones that were the most satisfying, the most characteristic of who you think you are.

Next, write a paragraph about each of the seven accomplishments, describing what you did well and how it made you feel. Note the skills that you demonstrated in each circumstance. As you go through the stories, you'll notice remarkable overlap between them. The qualities that you've always taken for granted will most likely turn out to be qualities that lead to your greatest successes. We often don't give ourselves credit for certain skills because they've always just been part of who we are.

Finally, you can start to see how those skills add up to a personality profile by asking yourself a few questions on the basis of these stories: What kind of environment do I thrive in? What kind of projects do I like to work on? What skills do I enjoy using most? When am I most proud of myself?

For example, Wendleton recalls that she spent some of her happiest childhood moments orchestrating big theater productions in her neighborhood. She wrote the plays, sold the tickets, made the costumes, mixed the lemonade, and starred in the show. Combining this memory with other positive experiences in her work and personal life, she learned that she loved "running the show" as a manager and an entrepreneur.

This exercise won't help you find your perfect job in the classified ads tomorrow, but it will give you a framework for understanding yourself. You'll know what you're looking for long term, and you can review different careers in the meantime on the basis of whether they fit a few, some, or most of the criteria you've outlined.

SHOULD I GO TO LAW SCHOOL?

Many graduate students see law school as the next-best option when they become frustrated with academia, but it's important to think through the consequences before you take the LSAT. Instead of asking yourself, "Do I want to go to law school?"—you should be asking, "Do I want to be a lawyer?" There's an enormous difference between the two experiences, and you should know what to expect from a law career before you spend three years and $100K earning the degree.

Because there are many kinds of lawyers, we interviewed two different people for their perspectives on the profession: Evan Wilson left academia after six years on the job market with a Ph.D. in English and chose the big-money, big-firm path after law school. Lola Zachary left her master's program in history without a degree and chose the low-paying public service path.

Q: Did you research law careers before starting law school?

Wilson: Before I applied to law school, I got a job as a word processor at a big law firm in New York. It was a good way to see whether I could bear the life.

Zachary: I worked as a paralegal after grad school. It opened my eyes to a whole field of work that I *don't* want to do—corporate law—and pushed me toward exploring different areas of the law that I now love: prosecution and litigation.

Q: What was your experience in law school?

Wilson: The weirdest part of law school was being back in a classroom where I was not only not in charge, but I was also the stupidest, most ill-prepared person in the room. I didn't realize you could get course outlines from other students—I wasted a lot of time doing unnecessary work.

Zachary: Law school is completely different from grad school. In my master's program, at least, everything was much fuzzier. Lots of "What do you think? What do you feel? What was the author trying to say?" In law school, it's much more concrete, much more structured.

Q: What area of the law interests you most, and why?

Wilson: I chose corporate tax almost by accident. I happened to get along with the corporate tax lawyers at my firm. They respect education; they're interested in books and opera—I could talk to them. Corporate tax is a more bookish area of law. It's more introverted.

Zachary: My favorite area of law is criminal prosecution. It's intense work, which a lot of corporate law is not. That has its benefits and drawbacks, obviously. You need to be very quick on your feet, know your law backward and forward, and be comfortable with public speaking.

Q: Do you use any of the skills you learned in graduate school in practicing law?

Wilson: Research is the skill I use most. Also, although I'm not at a level yet where my teaching skills are coming in handy, I hear that later a lot of what you do is teach complex tax codes to clients.

Zachary: I didn't use many of my skills from grad school as a paralegal. The only thing that might have applied was teaching. An ability to express myself clearly came in very handy when dealing with support staff, vendors, clients, and especially junior associates.

Q: How much debt do you have from law school, and how much money are you making now?

Wilson: My debt from law school is between $100,000 and $150,000. It's almost exactly equal to my first year's salary.

Zachary: I went into law school knowing that the jobs that I was interested in (prosecution or smaller litigation firms) wouldn't pay the big bucks. I'm $56,000 in debt. I had help from my family for the rest; otherwise, it would have easily been about $120,000. Since I'm only a law clerk this year, my salary isn't indicative of the legal market. I make somewhere between $40K and $45K. The jobs I'm applying to for next year only make between $50K and $70K.

Q: If you did it all over again, would you still go to graduate school?

Wilson: I'm glad I have a Ph.D. because I care about reading books and understanding them, but for me, that's a private thing. I don't have a vocation for teaching. I prefer working in the legal world. I'm much happier here—it's much more collegial than academe. I feel much more like people are pulling together. Academe had so many bitter fights over nothing.

Zachary: I don't really believe in changing anything. It sounds corny, but the road I took is the one I was supposed to take to get me here. If I finished my master's degree, instead of leaving without the degree, I might never have gone to law school. Working as a paralegal pushed me toward exploring different areas of the law that I now love.

The Bookstore at the End of the Mind

Many scholars would rather read than eat, sleep, or socialize. We're more at home in bookstores than at singles bars or barbecues. So let yourself travel to that imaginary bookstore at the end of the mind, the one with the big comfortable chairs and the good lighting. After you walk through the front door, glance at the best-seller table, and breathe in that new paper smell, which section of the store do you head for first?

Don't say "literary criticism" if you're an English Ph.D. or "medieval history" if you're a historian. Remember, this is the bookstore at the end of your mind. Nobody's watching—no classmates, no professors. Just you. So what section do you go to? And what book catches your eye?

If David Rosengarten, a former professor of theater history

at Skidmore, had done this exercise, he would find that he always headed straight for the cookbook aisle. A self-proclaimed lifelong "foodie," Rosengarten left academia to pursue a career in food writing that eventually led to his own nationally televised cooking show.

SHOULD I GO TO LIBRARY SCHOOL?
"Academic librarianship will be a natural fit for many Ph.D.'s in the humanities and social sciences, especially for those who are good at research," says Todd Gilman, a Ph.D. in English and an academic librarian at Yale University.

What are the best parts of being a librarian?
One of the greatest joys of library work is that I don't have to prepare lectures or grade papers but still make a meaningful contribution to college students' education.

What are the challenges of being a librarian?
One of the challenges is that academic librarians are generally held in lower esteem than the teaching faculty (by both the faculty themselves and the administration).

What kind of people do well in this field?
Generally speaking—and contrary to a popular stereotype, I might add—those who make the best librarians are the most outgoing. You have to really be devoted to service, whether it be to serve proactively on a reference desk, to provide excellent bibliographic instruction, to do collection development creatively, or even to be a great cataloger. Passivity and shyness will not get you very far. Enthusiasm and good people skills will.

What should a Ph.D. expect from library school?
It is difficult to generalize about library education. How good an experience you have depends mostly on the person teaching each particular class. The workload will seem light to me-

dium compared with most subject-specific programs at the better graduate schools.

Is library school expensive?

Most library school programs are dirt cheap because they belong to big state schools. And if there isn't a cheap library program near you, you can take the degree online and still get in-state tuition even if you are out-of-state in most cases. Also, there are a number of grants available specifically to Ph.D.'s who want to become librarians, offered, for example, by the Association of Research Libraries (ARL) and the Institute of Museum and Library Services (IMLS) in connection with specific library school programs.

What are the job prospects for librarians?

There are many would-be librarians with nothing more than a bachelor's degree and a master's in library science, and they are not in demand. But for subject specialists, like those with Ph.D.'s in English, foreign languages, history, art history, classics, economics, psychology, anthropology, and so on, the prospects are much better. Subject specialists make the best reference librarians, I believe, because of their thorough understanding of the research process. And their worth is recognized by many academic library search committees.

"This Is Your Brain on Graduate School"

What's going on in your head? What do you spend most of your time thinking about? Do you have interests and passions that crowd out what you're "supposed" to be doing? Are you spending too much time worrying about your adviser or your finances? Draw a map of your head, including all the clutter, and give each subject the proportional space it deserves. Be honest with yourself, but have fun.

Here's what a stereotypical graduate student's brain looks like:

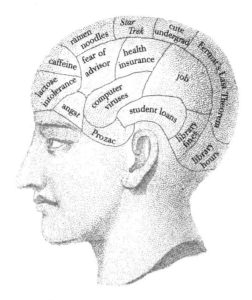

Now redraw your head. How would you like it to look? What do you want to spend your time thinking about?

No Need for a #2 Pencil

You've exhausted all the exercises in this chapter and still don't know what to do? Try a different approach. Instead of looking at your skills, try finding a job that matches your personality. Some of us were originally drawn to academic work because we love the solitary work of growing spores in petri dishes or rummaging through dusty archives. Others who thrive in a more collaborative environment may have come to grad school to pursue a love of teaching. Getting a different perspective on your strengths and weaknesses can help you narrow down your career choices.

Your university's career office probably offers some basic personality tests, but you can also find a wealth of free information on the Internet. Here are a few sites to try (because URLs change, be sure to visit our website at www.careersforphds.com for updated links):

Career Interests

http://career.missouri.edu/students/explore/thecareerinterestsgame.php
This simple but thorough game provides a wealth of information that helps you match your interests and skills with a similar career. You start by answering questions about your interests, hobbies, abilities, and values. You are scored according to how you match up with the following six categories: Realistic, Investigative, Artistic, Social, Enterprising, and Conventional. Then you select jobs that interest you from these groups.

Keirsey Temperament Sorter

http://www.keirsey.com/
Based on Carl Jung's work on "psychological types," the Keirsey Temperament Sorter asks you a series of questions and sorts you into distinct temperament types: rational, idealist, artisan, guardian. Each of the groups is then divided into four variants—one of which will match your personality. The best part of the site is seeing the famous people who match your psychological type.

Myers-Briggs Type Indicator

http://www.personalitytest.net/types/index.htm
You may have already taken this popular personality test at some point in your life. But you can take it with your workplace personality in mind, and you may find some new results. Answer sixty-eight multiple-choice questions to see where you land in the scale of the following traits: introvert/extrovert, intuition/sensation, feeling/thinking, perceiving/judging.

Job Hunter's Bible

http://www.jobhuntersbible.com/
Check out the online companion to Dick Bolles's popular career book *What Color Is Your Parachute?* to find links to a multitude of personality test sites as well as some interesting discussion of their uses and limitations.

No test is 100 percent accurate, but taking several of them can give you a better idea of your talents. Also remember that web tests tend to be more simplified than printed versions of these tests—so if you find them helpful, seek out more detailed information from a library or career resource center.

Where Are All Those Ph.D.'s Anyway?

Now that you've taken an inventory of your skills, likes, and dislikes, it's time to start thinking about where you can put them to use. Where do Ph.D.'s work outside the academy? Everywhere. "Scratch the surface of any major company and you'll find some Ph.D.'s," assures Carol Barash, former professor and founder of her own advertising agency.

What follows is a roundup of Ph.D.'s employed in fields from arts administration, to consulting, to government, to media, to technology. Because you may not know many people working outside the academy, these descriptions are designed to help you imagine other lives.

Nonprofits

Many former academics seek out nonprofit organizations as their first step outside academia. The culture of nonprofits can be particularly Ph.D.-friendly, since many share values similar to those of universities. But beware: Don't imagine that by going to a nonprofit you're escaping from the world of money. As one Ph.D. who worked as a nonprofit administrator cautions, "Nonprofits are just as worried about money as for-profit companies. They just have less of it."

Alyssa Picard, Ph.D. History, Labor Negotiator for a Teachers' Union

Alyssa Picard spent a great deal of time working with her union while a grad student at the University of Michigan. As she finished her degree and went on the academic market, she realized that what she valued most about grad school was that it caused her to "start thinking about why I'd had the opportunities I had, and about what would be the best use of my privilege to increase

the odds for others." She is now a labor negotiator and orga-
nizer for a teachers' union in Michigan. "I love helping people
overcome their fears in order to create positive change in their
work lives and in politics," Picard says. "I probably do more of
the kind of teaching I really like in this job than I ever did in a
classroom."

Lynn Davey, Ph.D. Psychology, Director, Maine Children's Alliance
Frustrated by the working conditions at the small college where
she was chair of the psychology department, Lynn Davey left
her faculty position to work for the Maine Children's Alliance, a
nonprofit advocacy group funded by the Annie E. Casey Foundation. She draws upon her scholarly research on early childhood education in her new position as director of an annual survey of the well-being of Maine's children.

Leslie Minot, A.B.D. English, Self-Employed Grant Writer
"I use my research skills, my writing skills, and my understanding of rhetoric to make a palpable material difference in the resources available to some wonderful nonprofit organizations in
the struggle for social justice and human rights. It wasn't a question of selling out, but of recognizing other things that also mat-
tered deeply to me."

Arts Administration

A love of the arts has motivated countless students to pursue careers in academia. But many have discovered that there are more
ways of supporting the arts than teaching them in a university.

**April Lynn James, Ph.D. Music, Mezzo-Soprano and Director of
The Maria Antonia Project**
April Lynn James embarked on a graduate career because of
her passion for baroque music and the misguided notion that "a
Ph.D. would secure me a career that paid well and would be eas-
ier to pursue than a music performance career." After complet-

ing a dissertation on the music and life of Maria Antonia, Electress of Saxony (1724–1780), she "gave up on trying to obtain a teaching position because I discovered that I disliked teaching and everything that went along with it. When I discuss this with some of my dear faculty mentors, they exclaim, 'But teaching is just like performing!' No. It is not. Audiences applaud (one hopes) when you finish performing. Students do not." Instead she has a part-time job with the Social Science Research Council working with their Mellon Mays Undergraduate Fellows program and has launched her own opera company, The Maria Antonia Project.

Carole Sargent, Ph.D. English, Literary Consultant and the President of A Word in Time

After completing her dissertation in eighteenth-century literature, Carole Sargent fulfilled her lifelong dream of becoming an author by pitching and selling a book to a well-known trade publisher. After publishing her first book, she worked as an adjunct at a few universities and continued writing. After several years she "decided to launch myself as a literary consultant rather than seek further academic work. It was *much* more lucrative, and soon I was earning many times what I had made as a professor." Now she works with authors to help them get ready to present their work to top publishers and find agents if they want them.

Margit Dementi, Ph.D. Comparative Literature, Executive Director of Seattle Arts & Lectures

Margit Dementi is the executive director of Seattle Arts & Lectures, a nonprofit literary organization. She is responsible for the artistic direction of a variety of programs, including the Poetry Series, Teachers as Scholars, and Wednesday University (a series of courses in the humanities open to the public). She most enjoys "knowing that what I do makes our community more interesting culturally and artistically and provides valuable educational opportunities to students and teachers."

Publishing and Media

People who especially love working with language may find careers in the publishing and media fields a natural fit. Companies always need writers who can develop a message and deliver it effectively. Many alums in these fields report that having a broad and diverse audience for their writing is extremely satisfying.

Gerald Tyson, Ph.D. English, Senior Editor at the National Environmental Trust

When he left a position as a professor at the University of Maryland in 1975, Jerry Tyson feared that he knew how to do only one thing: teach. "In fact, I had learned something much more valuable. I had learned how to learn," Tyson explains. He now works as senior editor for an environmental group. "Subsequently, I have learned never to 'throw away' a skill. Everything you do in one job can translate to some new opportunity or challenge for another."

Tony Russo, Ph.D. Psychology, CEO of Noonan Russo Communications

Tony Russo cofounded a New York public relations firm that specializes in representing pharmaceutical and biotechnology companies. He frequently hires science Ph.D.'s because he values their scientific expertise, but they have to be willing to start at the bottom, he warns. A successful job candidate at his firm must be able to write well, learn quickly, and juggle multiple clients and projects with grace.

James Levine, Ph.D. Education, Founder of Levine Greenberg Literary Agency

James Levine founded his own literary agency after a varied career in early childhood education and university administration. Representing authors is like coaching graduate students, but with the advantage that "I get to pick my students," as he says. Levine also fulfills his interest in research by running the

Families and Work Institute, located across the street from his agency, at the same time.

Teaching

Ph.D.'s who realize that they are born teachers probably won't be happy anywhere but in a classroom. Remember, however, that you can expand your definition of classroom beyond the boundaries of an undergraduate lecture hall. You may gain just as much satisfaction teaching high school students, corporate clients, community groups, or adult learners.

Bryan Garman, Ph.D. American Studies, Head of Wilmington Friends School

Bryan Garman enjoys the opportunity to "educate the whole student" but cautions that only people who truly love to teach should take on this kind of challenge. For academics applying to high schools, Garman recommends downplaying your scholarly research and limiting your use of jargon. The best candidates for high school teaching are those with fairly traditional fields of study (American history, rather than cultural studies) and some previous experience teaching adolescents, he advises.

Anna Patchias, Ph.D. English, Executive Director and Owner of Champion Tutoring

Anna Patchias began working for Champion Tutoring to earn extra money while she was in graduate school at the University of Virginia. Tutoring paid better than being a teaching assistant, and as she become increasingly disillusioned with academia, she devoted more time to tutoring, eventually becoming the executive director and finally purchasing the company from the founder when she decided to retire.

University Administration

For those of you who don't want to stray far from campus (or are limited by a spouse's job), academic administration can offer some of the same perks as teaching. You're still involved with the life of a university but have the opportunity to move outside the confines of your classroom. And while some university administration positions (in career centers or centers for teaching and learning, for example) may not require a Ph.D., you can be confident that a university employer will appreciate the value of your advanced degree.

Richard Bennett, Ph.D. Comparative Literature, Senior Associate Director of Leadership Gifts at Princeton University

Richard Bennett decided not to go on the academic market after finishing his degree "because I wanted to have control over where I lived and because I wanted to be exposed to a broader array of issues and concerns in my career than I perceived success in my field to permit." He got his first job, running the Woodrow Wilson National Fellowship Foundation's "Humanities at Work" program, by networking. While there, he had the opportunity to move into a development/fund-raising role and discovered that he enjoyed it. "There is no doubt that my knowledge of the university in particular and higher education in general is extremely helpful in my current role. It enables me to communicate with faculty members and administrators and also gives me a certain level of credibility both among colleagues and with prospective donors. Insofar as completing a Ph.D. can require a certain entrepreneurial drive, I would say that has also been valuable to me in my work."

Rebecca Bryant, Ph.D. Musicology, Director, Career Services and External Relations, The Graduate College, University of Illinois at Urbana-Champaign

Rebecca Bryant started pursuing a career in university administration even before finishing her dissertation on the impact of Progressive era reform on music in 1910s/1920s Chicago. She likes being in a university "filled with intelligent people and . . . a diversity of fascinating ideas" but prefers working as an administrator rather than a faculty member because "it suits my planning and organizational strengths, it provides me with more variety in my work, and it suits my lifestyle choices."

Government

Academics have found satisfying work in almost all offices of federal and state government, from the Smithsonian Institution to the National Park Service. Many of those we interviewed encourage candidates to persevere, since government hiring requires several months, many forms, and lots of patience to complete.

Julia Huston Nguyen, Ph.D. History, Senior Program Officer at the National Endowment for the Humanities (NEH)

Julia Huston Nguyen left a tenure-track position at a large university because while she loved historical research and writing, she found that teaching was not an activity she could see herself doing for several years. While "teaching introductory U.S. history to 100 or 150 undergraduates, many of whom resented the state's requirement that they take the course," she came across "a job ad from the NEH, sent in an application, and (several long months later) received an offer."

"I may still be in the honeymoon stage," she explains, "but I love my new job. I work in an office full of humanities Ph.D.'s, so I have found that vibrant intellectual environment outside the academy. I love being a generalist again. I get to read proposals from every discipline in the humanities, which is a window to some of the newest and best work that's being done. I also like feeling that my work is really helping people. I help applicants get funded, and those grants do a great deal of good for teachers and college/university faculty."

Alexandra Lord, Ph.D. History, Staff Historian for the U.S. Public Health Service

Alexandra Lord's interest in the history of medicine helped her win a position as a staff historian for a federal government agency. She describes her work as drawing heavily on her research skills. "We answer questions from the general public, from filmmakers, reporters, congressmen and congresswomen, policy makers, physicians, and scientists." After the drudgery of teaching the same classes over and over again as a professor, she finds the work constantly challenging. She also enjoys working with non-historians. "My work is done now with a view to a wider audience, and I publish not simply in academic journals but in non-academic places as well. This is what I dreamt about doing in academia, so it's a great fit for me."

Kay Atkinson King, Ph.D. Linguistics, Democratic Senior Policy Adviser to the Committee on International Relations of the U.S. House of Representatives

After completing her Ph.D., Kay Atkinson King spent several years raising her children and teaching part-time before embarking on a second career in government. When she received her first job offer with the U.S. House of Representatives, her initial reaction "was that I didn't have the right college degree." But after a few months on the job, she realized just how transferable her skills were. "Since my new congressional job dealt heavily with international relations, my linguistics background . . . and extensive travel gave me a greater understanding of cultures, ideas, and issues."

Research

Some graduate students and faculty members live for research. If this describes you, consider a career that will let you use your highly developed skills on a daily basis.

John Rumm, Ph.D. History, Researcher at History Associates

Researching the mysterious founder of the 125-year-old Burpee seed company, using historical records to suggest a new marketing strategy for Sears, Roebuck and Co., and helping the Special Olympics develop a Hall of Fame exhibit are a few of the diverse projects John Rumm has pursued at History Associates. His firm hires smart liberal arts graduates from all fields for work in archival research, litigation research, and corporate history research. The fifty-member firm produces oral histories, photo histories, and museum exhibits for client companies.

Sharyl Nass, Ph.D. Cell and Tumor Biology, Policy Analyst at the Institute of Medicine
While doing a postdoctoral fellowship, Sharyl Nass was active in the Johns Hopkins Postdoctoral Association, where she drafted a policy proposal for postdoctoral training. The combination of this experience and some savvy networking led her to a science policy position at the Institute of Medicine, which advises the president on health policy. Frustrated by the "grueling academic career track," she now researches and writes about cancer prevention and treatment. Being a policy analyst allows her to "function as a lifelong graduate student but earn a living wage with good benefits."

Consulting

It's a trade-off. Consulting offers some great intellectual challenges and pays extremely well, but be prepared for life on the road. Most consultants travel extensively, often spending the week at the client company and flying home on weekends, for months at a time.

Josh Fost, Ph.D. Neurobiology, Consultant for Thomson Consulting
Josh Fost became disillusioned with academia during his postdoctoral fellowship. He applied to computer programming jobs by posting his résumé on recruiting websites and was called by a headhunter who got him an interview with an information technology firm, Thomson Consulting. "When I interviewed, I tried to argue (although I wasn't sure I believed it at the time) that they needed people with general smarts and all-around analytical ability, who can build a logical structure around new situations," he remembers. "To my amazement, it turned out to be true!"

Emily Hill, Ph.D. History, Consultant for McKinsey & Company
Emily Hill sees a strong parallel between the skills needed in academia and in consulting. "In grad school I learned to deal with chaos, to make sense of the nonsensical. You learn to take

a huge pile of evidence and turn it into a story. In consulting, you're not even sure what the problem is much of the time, just that you have to fix it. It's just like a dissertation: you have to figure out what the right questions are. And then you need to show evidence, create a narrative—that's what academics and consultants do."

Ann Kirschner, Ph.D. English, President of Comma International

Ann Kirschner jumped on the new media trend early. Rather than let an academic job take her far from New York after finishing her doctorate, she answered a classified ad and started out in the world of cable television. That position put her at the forefront of Internet technology, which she parlayed into a job as founder and CEO of the National Football League's website, NFL.com. She took that experience back into the academy as head of Morningside Ventures, a for-profit Internet company created by Columbia University. Now she serves as president of Comma International, a consulting firm specializing in interactive media and education.

Technology Companies

Many Ph.D.'s have found challenging work in the technology sector. And it's not just math and computer science grads who thrive in tech careers; humanities and social science scholars are also skilled at learning the language of technology.

Geoff Davis, Ph.D. Applied Mathematics, Researcher at Microsoft Corporation

Geoff Davis took a leave of absence from his post as an assistant professor at Dartmouth for a one-year assignment at Microsoft. "After a great deal of soul-searching," he decided to quit his academic job. "I decided that I was more interested in having people use the results of my research than in writing lots of papers. (I should emphasize that I do still write papers, but it's no longer the primary focus of my activities.) I'm currently doing research on ways to improve Microsoft's digital audio player. To put things in perspective, maybe a hundred or so people read my most recent paper. The last Windows Media Audio player, on the other hand, was downloaded by two million people on the day it came out and was recently estimated to have forty million users."

Peter J. Stokes, Ph.D. English, Consultant for Eduventures.com LLC

A former instructor at Tufts, Peter Stokes's first job in the business world was with Datatech, a high-tech market research firm. A year later he moved to Eduventures.com, a consulting company for the for-profit education industry. "Start by identifying what it is you love to do. That's the only career worth fighting for," he advises. "And since you're going to have to fight for everything you get no matter which direction you head off in, you want to make sure it's worth the trouble."

Create Your Own Possibilities

These alumni profiles are just a small sample of the possibilities that are open to you. We hope we've helped jump-start your imagination. Now it's up to you to find out more about the fields that interest you. In the next chapter, you'll learn how to expand the options we've listed above by conducting information interviews with alumni and doing informal internships. As you learn more about how other people have organized their careers around their skills and interests, you'll develop a stronger sense of what's right for you.

....

POST-ACADEMIC PROFILE: DAVID ROSENGARTEN, TELEVISION COOKING SHOW HOST, PH.D. IN THEATER HISTORY

Hosting a nationally syndicated cooking show is the perfect blend of theater and teaching for David Rosengarten. Although he never imagined he'd find himself the host of the TV Food Network show *Taste*, he was unknowingly preparing himself for the job for many years.

Rosengarten had initially entered grad school with the goal of "directing theater and making a living at the same time." He finished his degree in four years and found a tenure-track job at Skidmore College in 1980. "I was glad to start at Skidmore because I thought I'd be free of the departmental politics that I witnessed as a grad student, but instead I discovered that I was in the battle, not on the sidelines," he remembers.

During his three years at Skidmore, Rosengarten also became disillusioned with college teaching. "During the early Reagan years, the freshmen didn't want to take any liberal arts courses. They only wanted to take business," he says. Rosengarten was "reasonably sure" that he was a good teacher and frustrated by students who didn't share his love of theater.

While walking past a cooking store one day, he noticed they were hiring people to teach classes. A lifelong "foodie," Rosengarten applied immediately. He did a cooking demonstration as an audition—garlic shrimp—and was hired. Rosengarten soon discovered that his cooking students, unlike his Skidmore students, "were full of passion and excitement. It was much more fulfilling."

Inspired by his new career direction, Rosengarten left Skidmore to pursue freelance writing full-time. He sold his first piece (on balsamic vinegar) to *Gourmet* in 1983 and ended up working as the magazine's restaurant reviewer. More recent projects include *The Dean & DeLuca Cookbook* and the award-winning cookbook *Taste,* based on his TV cooking show.

When the TV Food Network came along, Rosengarten says, "it was perfect for me. Teaching is great training for being on TV. I try to theatricalize food on my show; it's similar to the teaching I did at Skidmore. And like any other kind of teaching, the student-teacher interaction is the best part."

3 Testing the Waters

Networking and Transitional Experience

Kay Atkinson King took the long road to her job as senior policy adviser to the Committee on International Relations of the U.S. House of Representatives. She was offered an academic job when finishing her doctorate in linguistics at UCLA but turned it down to move to Germany with her new husband, who had just taken an academic job there. Although they planned to spend only one year in Munich, it was seven years and two sons later before they returned to the United States so her husband could take a job in Washington, D.C.

She tried to keep a hand in the academic field while raising her children and continuing to move around for her husband's career, but many of her attempts failed to launch. She cobbled together a series of part-time adjunct positions and research projects but found it hard to compete against colleagues who worked full-time. Eventually she came to the conclusion that "in putting my linguistics career on hold, I had chosen to give it up."

One evening at a dinner party, she had a long conversation with one of her husband's colleagues. The man was the son-in-law of a Democratic congressman and eventually encouraged her to apply for a job on Capitol Hill. Although her "first reaction was that I didn't have the right college degree," one year later she ended up getting a one-day-a-week legislative position in the office of the man's father-in-law.

It didn't take her or her colleagues long to realize that the skills she had developed in graduate school—like writing, re-searching, and analyzing—were transferable to other subjects. She moved from working one day a week to a full-time international relations position (and later a chief of staff job) with the congressman where her linguistics background and time in Europe proved immensely useful. "On Capitol Hill you deal with multiple areas, not just one specialization like in graduate school. But because I knew how to do research, I could become conversant very quickly no matter how often the subject matter changed."

You might think she just got lucky enough to sit next to the right person at a dinner party, but she suggests otherwise. "You have to be wise enough to grab chances when they happen," she advises. "I fostered many friendships and always asked people what they did" during the years she spent at home with her young children, she explains. When exploring careers, "graduate students need to go to many people just like they go to many books," she urges.

They also need to think about the skills they possess rather than just the subject area they've mastered. "Washington is full of lawyers who don't work as attorneys. Instead they use their legal educations in a wide variety of jobs. The same should be true of Ph.D.'s: we develop tremendous critical thinking and research skills that are transferable to so many jobs."

King's story illustrates some key points about post-academic job searches:

First, be open to unexpected possibilities. Some choices are shaped by necessity, not by desire. But remain open to the choices nonetheless. King had no idea she would end up on Capitol Hill when she embarked on an academic career. But now that she's there, she treasures the chance to focus on "issues of intolerance, discrimination, persecution, and religious liberty," some of the same issues she considered in graduate school. Don't be afraid to risk taking a job you never imagined. If you don't like it, you can quit. But you may find more satisfaction than you ever anticipated. We're always told to follow our dreams. But it can be detrimental to become so obsessed with one particular dream that you turn down other opportunities. Job hunting is full of serendipity and kismet. You can't control kismet, but there are some things you can do to help these cosmic forces along. As Branch Rickey, former manager of the Brooklyn Dodgers, once said, "Luck is the residue of good design."

Second, you have to research opportunities, not in a library or lab, but by picking up the phone and contacting anyone who might be able to help. Talk to the person sitting next to you at a dinner party—or at the gym, or in the PTA meeting at your kid's school. And although you must be open to chance, don't leave your search to chance alone. Pursue contacts who work in fields that appeal to you to see what they really do all day.

Third, you may need to take a temporary or part-time position to bolster your credentials. (This is what we mean by an internship: any kind of formal or informal, paid or unpaid experience that introduces you to a new field.) Don't be afraid to take something that seems less prestigious than being a tenure-track professor—like Kay King's first job on Capitol Hill. You have to be realistic. Even with an advanced degree, if you have no experience, you will probably have to start low. The good news is that you can move up quickly. A common feature of stories alumni told us was that their ability to learn helped them advance faster than their peers.

Fourth, be patient. You may not want to hear us encouraging patience. (We certainly didn't want to hear it when we were looking for jobs.) After spending years in graduate school, you probably feel like you need to get on with the rest of your life as quickly as possible. But even though we've condensed King's story in a few paragraphs, it took her twenty years on Capitol Hill to get where she is today—and several more years of adjuncting and part-time work before that. Although family circumstances and motherhood slowed down her career search, you should still be prepared to spend time building your career, regardless of your personal circumstances. The good news about King's

"THE WISDOM OF STARTING AT THE BOTTOM"

When Tony Russo got his first job on Wall Street, he thought that having a Ph.D. in psychology should count in his favor, that he should at least make a little extra money. "They quickly disabused me of that notion, and it was a hard pill to swallow," he remembers. "I told them I'd spent eight years in grad school, and they said that they were glad to have me, but the degree didn't count" as relevant experience.

Russo now sits on the other side of the hiring desk and finds that he shares the view of his former employers. As he interviews Ph.D.'s for jobs at the biotech/health care public relations firm he cofounded, Russo cautions job applicants that "if they want to switch careers, they will have to pay their dues." He looks for people who are not arrogant about their abilities. No matter how impressive their academic credentials, new hires must be willing to learn public relations from the ground up, and that often means starting with a lower salary than they expect.

However, there's an advantage to starting out at the bottom, Russo explains. "If you only have the skills for a $30K per year job, you shouldn't be in a $50K per year job. The employer will have unrealistic expectations for you, you'll miss out on learning fundamental skills, and others in the company will resent your leapfrogging over them." But if you start low, you can move up quickly and have a string of successes, Russo explains. "We've promoted people within six weeks," he adds.

story, however, is that it shows that it's never too late to embark on meaningful work. Even though she chose to spend several years raising children after completing her doctorate, she still was able to craft a meaningful career in government.

Finally, try to maintain a positive attitude. It's natural to want to rage against the circumstances that block you from pursuing an academic career—whether it's a tight job market, geographic limitations, financial constraints, or the family circumstances that shaped King's early career. And it's healthy for you to vent that rage; write it down, share it with your partner or close friends. But don't let it dominate your life. The most success-ful people we interviewed were those who had made peace with their conditions, which left them open to pursue new oppor-tunities. The rest of this chapter outlines some ways to design your job search that will help you create those opportunities.

The Power of Networking

Networking doesn't come naturally to many graduate students. (You might even cringe at the word itself because it sounds like a business cliché.) Jennifer Stone Gonzalez, a Ph.D. in commu-nications who took an internship at a telecommunications com-pany in order to jump-start her career, explains why some grad-uate students find it hard to network:

> In the business world, the most important information flows through people, not texts. Most of what you learn in business comes from informal dialogue, whether in person, on the phone, or via e-mail. This is one reason why people in the business world work so hard to establish interpersonal alliances. People in the business world read so they can cull information for use in conversations that fuel this exchange of learning and solve prac-tical problems.

Even if you don't like the word *networking,* you need to accept the concept. Books can help you research jobs, but they can't hire you, so you need to start building human connections.

Once you've determined one or two major fields of inter-est (see the previous chapter for exercises to help narrow your choices), write down on separate index cards the names of any-one you can think of who works in those fields. Seek out for-mer academics who'll understand your position, but don't limit yourself only to them. You don't actually have to *know* these people. You'll need lots of names, so don't worry about weeding out anyone now. It doesn't matter if they are high-level or low-level employees, if they have lots of experience or little. Just start some momentum. Don't worry if you don't know anyone in your field now, because next you're going to expand your range of contacts. Trust us on this. We found all the people profiled in this book by expanding our network and asking everyone we knew for help.

- Ask your family about their friends, old schoolmates, old boyfriends or girlfriends, friends of friends, and old family friends.
- Ask your friends about the same list of people above; don't discount anyone. You never know who might be able to help you.
- Ask university staff members, such as your favorite librarian or that guy who always helps you out at the computer center, about their friends and families. Who do they know?
- Ask casual acquaintances and associates for help.
- Go to the alumni office at your university and search for potential contacts. Keep an eye on the class notes in the back of the alumni magazine; it's a great place to find detailed information about where people work and how to reach them. Don't be shy about contacting undergrad alumni. Many universities have alumni Listservs that post announcements about jobs; be sure to sign up for as many as possible.
- See what your university's career office has to offer. Some universities (like Harvard and the University of Chicago) are well-equipped to help graduate students and professors make a change, while others are more focused on placing undergraduates. Either way, you can't afford to pass up some free career counseling.
- Go to campus recruiting sessions for companies that interest you and get business cards from the recruiters. You may not be ready to apply to the company, but you can always write to them afterward and ask for an information interview. As Kim Dixon, a Ph.D. in theater and drama who now works in advertising, recalls: "I got very little guidance from my program (a halfhearted evening where a few post-academics came and talked about what they were doing; this came a few months before my defense, after several other students

had already defected). I found my job by using the university's *undergrad* career resources—counselors, tests, job fairs. I started having informational interviews with ad agencies after going up to a panelist after a job fair and explaining that I wasn't an undergrad but was looking for a job that acknowledged my experience and maturity; one of those interviews eventually turned into a job offer."

- When you see mention of someone interesting in a newspaper or magazine article, get their contact information and add it to your cards. People are usually flattered that someone read the article about them so carefully.
- If you've ever done summer jobs or volunteer work in your field of interest, call up former supervisors or coworkers and ask about contacts.
- Every time you talk to someone in an information interview, ask them for more names. You'll eventually end up talking to people removed by three or four degrees of separation.

You should have a stack of index cards by now. Hang on to them. As you get going, you'll fill in contact information (phone, address, fax, e-mail) on each person. You'll also want to make notes on the back of the card about your conversation, such as to whom they referred you and other key points.

Networking That Works

Even after you've gathered a stack of names, networking systematically may feel a little pushy or awkward. Try these networking techniques—one for when you know what you want to do, and one for when you're still trying to figure out how to do what you love.

If You Have a Specific Goal

Let's say you're hooked on *Antiques Roadshow* and you want to work for Sotheby's auction house.

- Go to the Sotheby's website and dig around until you find a page of staff biographies—nearly every website has one somewhere. Or Google until you find some information.
- Pick a person to contact—maybe someone who went to your alma mater, someone with a grad degree, someone who works on your favorite period of American furniture, someone who also runs marathons. Any pretext is fine, though you won't always be able to find one.
- Then, e-mail the person directly with a very brief note stating your common interest and that you found them on the company website. Ask if they'd be willing to answer two questions via e-mail about breaking into the field. (Limiting it to two reassures them that you won't take much time.) Some won't respond, but many will.

We've spoken about this technique at graduate schools across the country. Each time, we hear back from students who tried this technique and had answers in ten minutes. Of course, that doesn't mean you can land a job in ten minutes—but you can start building contacts, which is an essential first step.

If You're Trying to Figure Out What You Want to Do

We borrowed the idea of the "gracious note" from a book by Carolyn See called *Making a Literary Life: Advice for Writers and Other Dreamers*. She requires her creative writing students to send short personal notes to three writers they admire. Whether you send your gracious note to a cookbook author, an entrepreneur, or your favorite commentator on NPR, make it to someone for whose work you have a sincere enthusiasm.

The gracious note is only about three sentences long: one to introduce yourself, one to compliment their work, one to say you're looking forward to seeing what they do next. The gracious note does not ask for anything. In some cases, people receive lovely, inspirational letters in response to their gracious notes and begin a correspondence. Many times they receive nothing.

While it may seem desperately New Agey, we nonetheless believe that the act of writing a gracious note is the first step in bridging the distance between your dreams and your reality. Even if seems hokey to you, it's at the very least a place to start. Just keeping a list of the people and places that inspire you to write a gracious notes is data worth collecting.

Whatever technique you use, you'll likely find that the best and worst thing about networking is that you can't force it: it's rarely linear. Often you'll start pursuing one topic, but end up discovering something valuable but totally unexpected: "Well, I don't know any advertising firms that are hiring interns, but my brother runs a catering business and needs someone to copyedit his marketing materials."

Or someone will contact you months or even years after you've written them, saying, "Are you still interested in working here?" This actually happened to Sue. No kidding—she got a call from someone she had met two years earlier while networking and ended up landing the job. (See "Susan's Story" in the introduction for details.) In any case, when you network, your goal should be creating possibilities, not immediate results. If nothing else, it should take the pressure off to know that success is not defined as an immediate return.

Information Interviews

The notion of calling or sitting down with a stranger to talk about careers probably sounds completely foreign to you. University job hunters don't do this stuff. Why? Because every grad student sees firsthand what an assistant professor's job looks like. That's what being a teaching assistant is all about. You see the pitfalls and perks in advance, and you develop a sense of what's needed to be successful in that career.

You probably also see professors much differently than you did when you were an undergraduate. Maybe as an undergraduate you thought professors had it easy—they slept late, only worked a few hours a day, just made up lectures as they went along. But now that you've been a teaching assistant or a faculty member, you can see up close how many hours professors work on their publications in order to get tenure, how contentious academic politics can be, and how daunting and time-consuming grading a mountain of term papers is.

While grad school allows you to see all sides of a professor's life, that kind of multiple-year apprenticeship just isn't practical when you're trying to figure out how to change careers. That's where the information interview comes in. It's an accelerated crash course in what it's like to be in someone else's shoes. For Jorge Pedraza, a comparative literature professor who decided to pursue a career in management consulting, information interviewing became "a kind of mini-M.B.A. program," in which he learned not only about a field that interested him but also about navigating the interview process itself. Interestingly enough, his training in European languages proved to be a great asset. Researching management consulting firms "was all about learning to speak their language," he explains. "It's just like learning French or Spanish or German."

While the whole idea of information interviewing may feel like a foreign language to you, it is absolutely the best way for you to research other careers. Since you have probably been surrounded by university people for the last few years, your perspective on how stockbrokers, engineers, high school teachers, entrepreneurs, and everyone else spends their day is bound to be a little vague. Here's your chance to separate out what you *think* you'd love to do from what you want to do.

And the best news is that you can start anytime. Whenever you feel that you're curious about a career ("Hey, I bet I'd look pretty good in that surveyor's jumpsuit!"), you can follow our advice below and set up an information interview. There's no commitment. You don't need to be ready to abandon academia or have your résumé perfectly polished. In fact, it's best if you're not immediately desperate for a job, because, as we'll explain, you're not allowed to ask anyone to hire you when you're information interviewing. You just need an open mind, some basic manners, and a willingness to listen.

An information interview is a cross between a dress rehearsal and a reconnaissance mission. You need to keep your eyes and ears open, while presenting yourself in the best possible light; it can be a tricky balancing act. But don't worry. We'll explain in this section the etiquette you need to follow in order to set up an interview, make a solid connection, and then follow up afterward.

Information Interview Etiquette

First and foremost, you can't ask anyone for a job. This may sound paradoxical, but it is the most important unwritten rule of information interviewing: *You must say explicitly that you are not looking for a job . . . yet.* That's the key. In order for someone to be willing to take the time to meet with you, you must in turn guarantee them that you will not put them in an embarrassing or awkward situation by asking them for a job.

Everyone you meet will know this rule. They are also aware that you are information interviewing because you will be job hunting *very, very soon,* but this social convention allows both of you to speak more freely. You can ask questions you would never bring up in an actual job interview; they can speak honestly about how they view your résumé and experience. More importantly, if assured that you aren't hitting them up for a job, the person you're interviewing will be inclined to look at you in broad terms ("Hmmm, sounds like she might really like public relations better than consulting—she should give Harry a call") instead of narrow ones ("Nope, we've got nothing for her here"). Anyone who has worked in one particular field for several years develops a strong sense of the kind of people who enjoy and are successful in their kind of work. You want to tap into that knowledge.

Setting Up the Information Interview

It's always safest to send a letter before calling someone for an information interview. It gives them a chance to decide how to respond, and it reassures you that the person will recognize your name when you call to follow up. Your letter should be short and to the point; keep your audience in mind. They don't want to know your entire life story or how conflicted you are about possibly leaving academia. They're busy; they just want to know what you want from them. Many of the graduate students we've met with have been surprised to see how many people agree to meet with them. Even people with extremely busy schedules like Kay King told us that they have been happy to meet with job searchers.

Your basic letter should (1) let them know how you found their name, (2) assure them that you are not asking them for a job, and (3) ask for an appointment in person or by phone. Some important features to note:

- If you're writing to a high-flying executive, it's usually best to say that you will call *their assistant* to make an appointment. It's fairly standard practice in the business world to have someone else keep your calendar once you reach a certain level, and you want to show that you know the right protocol. If they don't have an assistant, then you'll simply have flattered them.
- Be sure to specify how much time you want: thirty minutes is a good slot of time to suggest, but leave it open to the interviewee if they want to shorten or extend it.
- Keep discussion of yourself and your background to a minimum—a sentence or two at most. Remember that you're asking for an appointment to talk about *their* experience, not yours.

Here's a sample letter to give you an idea of the right tone:

Dear Ms. Lewis:

My [friend/neighbor/dentist's name] suggested that I contact you to find out about careers in public relations. I'm finishing my Ph.D. in sociology at Cornell and am interested in exploring careers outside of academia. I did all the publicity for Cornell's theater productions this year and would welcome the opportunity to talk with you about how one breaks into the field.

Would you be willing to meet with me for thirty minutes to discuss how you got started in public relations? I'd appreciate any advice you can offer—I'm not officially job hunting just yet. I'll contact your assistant next week to see if we can arrange a time.

Sincerely,
Erin Moran

When you call to follow up on this letter, keep it short and simple: "Hello, I'm calling for Ms. Lewis. This is Erin Moran. I'm following up on a letter I sent last week asking for an information interview about careers in public relations." Figure out whether you'll meet over the phone or in person, set up a time, and reconfirm before you hang up. Be as flexible in your time as possible; you want your interviewee to meet you when he or she isn't distracted by other commitments.

Before You Go to the Interview

- Research the company your sources work for, even if you don't think you'd want to work there, so you don't waste the person's time asking about what XYZ Corp. does.
- Print out several copies of your draft résumé so you can show them your experience quickly, and so they can offer you pointers.
- Consider getting business cards printed. They're cheap and they're the universal currency of the business world. People will always be giving you their cards—and if they can stick your card in their Rolodex (or scan it into their Palm Pilot), they're more likely to contact you when the perfect job comes along.
- Although talking at the person's office is usually most convenient, you may decide to meet elsewhere for coffee or lunch.

Remember that you should offer to pay since you initiated the meeting.

- Practice your two-minute introduction. See sample dialogue below.

What to Ask During an Information Interview

Regardless of whether you're talking to a sympathetic alum or your grandmother's chiropractor, you should start the conversation with your two-minute introduction, your synopsis of who you are and why you are here. It should be concise and upbeat, summarizing your past and indicating your future direction. Here are two examples:

"I'm finishing a dissertation on _____ and am starting to think about other careers. I've worked outside academia in _____ and found that I enjoy _____. I have strong _____ skills, and I'm exploring my options right now. Your field appeals to me because _____, and I want to learn more about it."

"I thought that your work seemed interesting because I have experience in _____, and think I would enjoy _____, but I'm interested in learning more. I'm not looking for a job quite yet, but I really appreciate your taking the time to talk with me about what's out there."

Ask the interviewee about his or her background:
- How did you get started in this field?
- What excites you about this kind of work?
- What do you like least?
- What's your average day like?
- What skills are important to have in this field?
- What is the entry-level position like?
- Would you do anything differently if you had to do it all again?

- What makes a résumé go to the top of the pile?
- How flexible are the criteria for jobs in this field?
- Can you suggest any other people I should talk to?

If you're interviewing a former academic, add these questions:
- Why did you leave academia?
- What did you study?
- What was your first job out of grad school?
- Do you use your academic skills in your work?
- Do you miss anything about academia?
- Did you have any idea when you left grad school that you'd end up in this place?
- How would you advise someone in my position?
- What have your classmates done with their careers?

If you have a draft résumé, this is a great time to take it out. It will save you from having to run down a chronology of your life, and you'll be able to take advantage of one of the greatest benefits of information interviewing: getting advice on revising your résumé from people who already work in the field you're trying to enter. Take advantage of this free counseling by asking if your interviewee can suggest any changes in content or format, offer ideas on skills you should highlight or downplay, identify any glaring holes in your experience, and suggest ways to build up what's missing.

What Not to Say During an Information Interview

Since you're there to learn about someone else's experience, don't talk too much about you. This includes your dissertation. One employer described to us an information interview with a graduate student who wanted to learn more about banking. However, the grad student spent most of the interview describing his dissertation on Nigeria's underground economy in such detail that the interviewer got lost. "About five minutes in, I just had no idea what she was talking about," he recalls. It's fine to briefly mention your area of research, but remember that even if someone asks questions about your subject, you should limit yourself to a few sentences.

On the other hand, don't apologize for your academic background or your lack of other experience. Earning or pursuing a graduate degree is something to be proud of; you just need to focus on the ways in which your training can help you thrive in a variety of environments. Try to keep your tone positive. Don't belabor your motives for entering or leaving academia or whine about the job market and your unreasonable advisers. Your goal is to learn as much as possible about a given career field, so don't waste your time (and your contact's) by losing focus.

As you shift the focus away from yourself, be sure to stay polite and interested. Graduate school teaches us to be critical and analytical. While these skills will serve you well in a variety of jobs, it's best to withhold any criticisms or observations about why you wouldn't like what they do during an information interview. No matter how sure you are that you would hate this person's job, remember that they may have other ideas or other contacts for you. Keep an open mind. (Remember, you have to leave yourself open to a little kismet.) The trick is to keep your expressions of enthusiasm sufficiently vague. Unless you're sure that you want to pursue a career in this person's field, giving the impression that you're extremely interested when you're still on the fence can lead to an awkward situation. They may offer specific help that you don't want to accept.

Words that should not come out of your mouth:
- I can't get an academic job so I'm going to have to do something else.
- What's the ideological positioning of your organization?
- I don't have any experience.
- I've been in school for ten years and am totally impractical.
- I can't imagine doing anything else.
- I'll die of boredom.
- I just want to get a job for a year so I can go on the market again.

- I don't think I could sit in a cubicle nine to five. How do you stand it?
- I have trouble with deadlines.
- I'm broke.
- How can you stand to work summers? How much vacation would I get?
- I don't think I could get up before 10 a.m.
- How much money do you make?

Wrapping Up the Information Interview

You should make sure to schedule your interview for a specific block of time, usually thirty minutes or less. But if your contact seems distracted or bored, change the subject and then offer to let them get back to work.

- As you end your appointment, say that you'll just ask one last question to let them know you're keeping to the schedule. Don't overstay your welcome.
- Leave them something with your name, phone, and e-mail on it—a draft of your résumé, a business card if you have one.
- Ask who else they would suggest you meet.
- Before you leave, politely reconfirm anything they've offered you (such as mailing you materials, digging up a phone number for you, reviewing your résumé) and thank them again.
- Ask if you can call on them in the future if you have other questions.
- Send a thank-you note the following day including a specific reference to your conversation.

Sample Thank-You Letter

Dear Ms. Lewis:

Thank you for meeting with me yesterday; it was great to hear your story. I was especially interested to learn about your work on behalf of the NAACP. I think social marketing may be the right area of PR for me. And it's always encouraging to hear from a former academic who is happy and successful in her new career.

I'm revising my résumé as you suggested—I appreciate the advice. I'll check with you next week to see if you've had a chance to find Larry Hagman's number—I look forward to talking with him.

Thanks again for taking the time to talk with me.

Sincerely,
Erin Moran

After the Information Interview

So you've scheduled five interviews and you still don't have anything to show for it. Now what? Don't be discouraged. You're not in this to get a job offer. Yet. The payoff for these meetings may come years down the road. Don't fail to follow up because you think you won't need to talk to the person again. You never know how this connection may help later on. Only one in five information interviews is truly interesting and useful; don't stop scheduling new appointments because you hit a few dead ends. Also, remember to separate the person from the field; you may not hit it off with someone, but you might still like the work.

Different Levels of Information Interviewing

Like everything else, your information interview skills improve with practice. So try to conduct your first interviews, those fuzzy "I'm still totally unsure what I want to do" conversations, with sympathetic listeners. Start with friends and family members and fellow alumni. Nick Corcodilos, who left the Stanford University graduate program in cognitive psychology to become a headhunter and career expert, advises that you "ask alumni all your initial questions. They are almost always glad to help. Ask them: 'What could I do with these skills?' 'How could I apply my skills in your field?' 'What would you do in my situation?' 'What's it like to work in your job?'"

Once you've begun to identify a field of interest, you can start to ask more specific questions. You'll probably be ready to take a first stab at a résumé (see the next chapter for advice) now that you have some target employers in mind. But don't get carried away: at this stage you're still there to learn. As one career-changing professor described it, setting up interviews requires "putting your ego in your pocket." "Know what you don't know," he advises, "and then use everything in your power to learn it."

After you've identified a particular job that you're targeting and have produced a strong résumé, you might want to ask some of your information interviewees if they would be willing to conduct a mock job interview with you. Different companies and industries conduct widely varied types of job interviews. Some organizations make decisions after talking to you for half an hour about your strengths and weakness while others put candidates through several rounds of standardized tests, problem-solving exercises, and one-on-one questioning before they make up their minds. Find out what the standard is in your field, and prepare yourself to meet the challenge.

Getting Your Feet Wet: Internships, Part-Time Jobs, and Volunteer Work

Even better than informational or mock interviews, internships (which we define as any kind of short-term learning experience) educate you about your field of interest and build your credentials. Volunteer work and part-time jobs are great ways to accomplish these goals. Immersing yourself in the field, even at an entry-level position, can help you figure out the right questions to ask. "It's important to spend time with the people in the industry to get to know how to behave, how to build the personal skills you need to network, and to learn the lingo," advises Nick Corcodilos. Former Harvard linguistics graduate student Samuel Birger agrees: "You've got to learn the idiolect." As founder of his own naming business, Birger credits his language training with helping him quickly learn the vocabulary of the business world.

Next summer, instead of breathing in toxic fumes in the lab or Xeroxing in some dark corner of the library, research your own life with an internship. What would it be like to work at an advertising agency? A publishing company? A hospital? An investment bank? A preschool? A restaurant? Since most on-campus summer jobs are pretty low paying, it's the perfect time to explore what your town can offer. An internship is a great way to get to know another field, meet some different kinds of people, and gain a little perspective on your academic work.

According to Craig Williams, a Ph.D. in industrial psychology, internships are one of the many ways Ph.D.'s can keep their options open. As director of Employee Resources at Pfizer Pharmaceuticals, he sees numerous job candidates with Ph.D.'s in the sciences. "Keep one foot out of academia at all times," he counsels, "so you won't lose touch with the kinds of work offered in the business world. Don't expect your professors to understand or value your experience outside academia. Just do it anyway."

Volunteer work is an ideal way to learn about a new field—who can refuse to hire you when you'll work for free? Chemistry Ph.D. Robert Rich planned his exit from academia by volunteering in the field he wanted to enter. While doing a postdoc at the National Institutes of Health, he arranged with his adviser to spend one day a week volunteering in the office of science and policy programs at the American Association for the Advancement of Science. "This arrangement enabled me to pay my rent and also get my foot in the door." When a job opened at AAAS a few months later, "I was the natural choice," Rich says.

While Rich carefully planned his career transition via volunteering, other job hunters benefit unexpectedly from their pro bono work. When Rodney Whitlock was a graduate student in political science at the University of Georgia, he volunteered for U.S. Representative Charlie Norwood's campaign. Much to Whitlock's surprise, Norwood invited Whitlock to join his staff after he won the election, launching Whitlock's new career on Capitol Hill.

A CAUTIONARY TALE ABOUT NONPROFIT WORK

Rob Peters, a Stanford biology Ph.D. who has worked both in academia and in the nonprofit sector, sees some alarming similarities between the two worlds. "They're both dysfunctional and poorly managed," he says. "And they both use idealistic young people as their fuel."

During the years he worked for a large, well-known environmental group in Washington, D.C., Peters became disillusioned with nonprofit organizations. One of the biggest problems, he says, is that nonprofits have little room for advancement. "You work eighty hours a week under tight deadlines for very low pay for years, and then there's nowhere to go," he warns. "It's almost like being an academic. You're an acolyte to the higher purpose." And as in academia, he says, the upper levels of nonprofits were fully staffed in the 1970s, and few positions are opening up. The organization he worked for even warned young staffers that "this isn't a career path; it's a place to get some experience."

So if nonprofit work is part of your short-term plan, you may be wise to ask questions about where this job will take you in the long term, such as: What kind of advancement opportunities does the group offer for someone who stays three to five years? What kind of career paths have previous employees taken? Where can I expect to go from here?

Temp work can also provide a crash course in another field. Try asking several different temp agencies to place you at a certain company that interests you. They know that offering a client a smart cookie like yourself is a real coup and will often go out of their way to accommodate you. And if you're temping in the right kind of company, people will realize quickly that you have a lot more to offer than your coffee-making skills. You can learn the business and make some contacts, not a bad deal for a month-long investment.

What's important to understand here is that we're talking about paying your dues for months, not years. The credentials and the skills associated with earning an M.A. or a Ph.D. will accelerate your career development enormously. You offer employers a written guarantee of your intelligence and diligence. A tiny bit of the most informal kind of experience—combined with outstanding academic credentials—opens doors. The Ph.D. alone won't get you the job, but it gives you the benefit of the doubt when combined with a small portion of relevant experience.

Transitional Tales

Paying your dues in a volunteer or part-time position may be painful—but it's necessary. Here are some stories of graduate alumni whose first jobs helped them realize that their dissertations were not their greatest accomplishment, but that their ability to think through mountains of information set them apart in careers outside the academy.

Dan Porterfield, Vice President for Public Affairs and Strategic Development, Georgetown University

In order to earn money while working on his English doctorate at New York University, Dan Porterfield worked as a speechwriter for the president of the university. He turned out to be quite good at speechwriting and ended up getting an offer to become a speechwriter for Secretary of Health and Human Services Donna Shalala. He hadn't even finished his dissertation yet, but he took the job as a once-in-a-lifetime opportunity. During the next few years, Shalala (a former university president) supported his efforts by giving him time off to finish his dissertation. His HHS experience led him to Georgetown University, where he now works as both VP for Public Affairs and as a professor in the English department. He enjoys his new post enormously because, he says, "I'm most happy at the crossroads between the university and the outside world."

Scott Emmons, Greeting Card Writer, Hallmark Cards

Although Scott Emmons enjoyed teaching classics at a small college in Kentucky, he had a dream of becoming a Hollywood screenwriter. He believed that he had the talent, but he had a family to support. How could he leave a tenure-track job for a long-shot prospect in Hollywood? So he developed a personal plan for breaking into the field. He built his portfolio by free-lancing as a gag writer for cartoonists. He made some money, got to know the business, and confirmed that he was headed in the right direction. After a year or two, he began to look for full-time humor writing jobs and decided that Hallmark offered the best chance for him to be creative while earning a steady pay-check. He's recognized throughout the company as one of their most creative and successful writers. Does he use his graduate education? Well, he says he learned to write humor by teaching Greek comedies. And he still does some Greek translation on the side to keep his language skills sharp.

So When Do I Start Looking for a Job?

Once you've conducted some information interviews and tried the waters with an internship or temporary position, it's proba-bly time to start looking for a specific job. But how do you know when? Remember, this is about kismet, so there's no one par-ticular moment when information interviews end and a more specific search begins. For most job seekers, the right positions become available as you learn to recognize them. There are, however, a few questions to ask yourself before you start trying to set up actual job interviews:

• Do you feel confident that you understand how the field works and that you have something to contribute?
• Do you know the title and requirements of the job you want?
• Is your résumé ready to be seen?

The next chapter will tell you everything you need to know to turn your CV into a résumé so you can get in touch with your information interviewees and internship contacts and let them know the hunt is on.

....

"I went to college at sixteen and finished grad school at twenty-five. I was a big nerd. I missed out on a lot," Shannon Mrksich says. As she started applying for postdocs, a friend who was an entertainment lawyer noticed an opening for a chemistry consultant at a law firm and urged her to apply. Her friend wrote up a résumé for her and sent it off, but Mrksich was convinced she would never get the job.

Not only did she get the job, but she loved it. While advising a legal team involved in a biotechnology patent dispute, Mrksich discovered that "I loved to write and I loved working with people instead of lab equipment. Who knew?" And she also had the satisfaction of seeing her chemistry expertise put to immediate, practical use.

But Mrksich admits that her conversion to post-academic life didn't happen overnight. In her first few months at the law firm, "I couldn't even work the copy machine. I had to relearn basic skills like stapling. But you can't find yourself in six months," she cautions. "It just takes a little longer." Soon Mrksich had mastered the basic office routine and begun studying for her law degree at night.

"Conventional wisdom says that going into industry is the fall-back position for scientists, but, really, industry is just like academia," Mrksich maintains. Once she stepped off campus, Mrksich was "amazed about the job opportunities that you never hear about." Chemists are going into consulting, investing, technical sales, technical writing, and other fields, she says. "Even the White House hires scientists" to explain technical matters that come up in policy debates.

Mrksich advises other graduate students that "it never hurts to look around. When I was in grad school, I had this idea that somehow the Chemistry Police were going to get me" if she dared think about jobs outside academia, she jokes. "You feel like a traitor for even considering other paths. But no one has to know you're looking."

4 This Might Hurt a Bit

Turning a CV into a Résumé

It's not about you. It's about the job.

The biggest difference between a résumé and a curriculum vitae (CV) is that a résumé focuses on the employer's needs, rather than explaining every detail of your credentials. Every time we help someone turn a CV into a résumé (and when we struggled with it ourselves), our advice always boils down to the same essential point: Your résumé has to teach the reader why you can do *this particular job*. This change in approach may not sound that large to you right now, but, done correctly, the process requires a seismic shift. You'll have to learn to see yourself in an entirely different way.

Résumé writing is not pleasant work. No one likes to remove all those hard-won publications and conference papers from their CV or condense years of teaching experience into a single line. Downplaying your academic credentials feels like failure. So why can't you just reorganize your CV and let employers figure out the rest for themselves? They can see you're smart enough to do whatever they need done, right? Wrong. If everyone else submits résumés that speak directly to the employer's needs, why should he or she spend extra time trying to puzzle out your credentials?

In addition, the range of candidates applying for any post-academic job is enormous compared to those who apply for academic jobs. For example, let's say that you're seeking a position as an assistant professor of political science. You know your competition well—other Ph.D.'s in the same field who have similar teaching and research experience. Your challenge in applying for this job is to make small differences in your intellectual approach stand out in a field of nearly identical candidates.

Now imagine yourself applying for a job as a researcher for a nonprofit group you admire. Sure, you have a Ph.D. in political science that shows you're a smart cookie and you've been a dues-paying member of the group for ages. But why should someone take the risk of hiring a person with zero experience? That's why your résumé has to be persuasive and relevant. You can't expect special treatment. You must reduce the risk of employing you by showing that you have done similar work before, that you have the right skills, that you understand their mission, and that you are eager to be a part of this group.

While all that may sound daunting, there is also some good news. First, your chance of getting the job is as good as anyone else's if you can make a convincing case for yourself. (We've heard a lot of stories about people flatly refusing to interview or hire Ph.D.'s, and it does happen from time to time. However, we've seen far more Ph.D.'s ruin their own chances by turning in a seven-page résumé or talking endlessly about their dissertations.) Second, your research and teaching skills can give you an advantage in your job hunting. Third, a Ph.D. after your name certainly helps your résumé get noticed. It also means that you can juggle evidence and construct an argument, which is exactly what you must do in your résumé and your cover letter.

Although we've said that you must show that you fit "this particular job," we don't mean that you have to contort yourself to fit the requirements of some vaguely interesting help-wanted ad. For now, your imagined audience should be any company or organization you've learned about through your research and networking.

Take note: It may take you several tries to develop a presentable résumé. Karen Rignall, a former graduate student in anthropology, recalls that her first attempts to turn her CV into a résumé were a bit misguided. "I looked back at my first résumé and it seemed so naive. I had made no effort to pare it down, to make it readable, even the font was hard to read. It looked like an academic paper and was clearly an academic talking, even though I was trying to stress the part-time jobs. It was wordy and looked awful visually."

For Rignall, the whole process of cataloging her achievements was gut-wrenching. Disheartened by several years of graduate study, her biggest problem was a lack of confidence. "I had a hard time accepting my accomplishments and conveying them in a résumé. It seemed immodest. I felt like I couldn't claim my earlier experiences: 'I don't really know how to do that.'" Eventually, a supportive friend who had left graduate school for the business world sat down and helped her present her achievements in an appropriate format, but the experience was still difficult. "She gave me good, constructive advice," Rignall recalls, "and I cried anyway." (You can see her final product on page 116.)

Getting Ready to Write a Résumé

You may have been so focused on the Big Three of the CV (scholarship, teaching, and service) for the past several years that you've forgotten why these categories exist in the first place: to please a particular audience. The Big Three are nothing more than a list of the qualities that are important to the committees that hire assistant professors. The Big Three do not define you. The Big Three are not your only skills. In fact, they may not even be your greatest strengths. Most grad students and professors are well aware that they are not equally gifted in all three areas. Let that knowledge free you from pretending to be someone you're not.

Look at your past experience from a different perspective, and then forge ahead and research a few companies that interest you.

Reimagine Your Past

Graduate school may have taught you to be harshly critical of yourself. Is there such a thing as a happy, confident graduate student? It's time to learn to see yourself outside of the graduate school mold. Let's start with your past.

First, make a laundry list of every activity you've ever done, including summer jobs, internships, hobbies, volunteer work, part-time gigs, big academic or administrative projects, and temp jobs. Everything counts. Now, describe each event in as many ways as possible. How would you describe that job to your neighbor? To a stranger on the subway? Step back and try to get a broader view of what you've done. Focus on being specific but not necessarily comprehensive in your descriptions.

Instead, pick out the most interesting and most relevant parts of the experience, and quantify whenever possible. How many people did you work with? What was the result of your work? How many months or years of experience did you gain? Did you have any ideas, however small, that made things work a little better around the office? What did you bring to the experience that the previous person did not? It may feel a little weird to highlight one detail of your summer job without contextualizing it alongside the rest of your duties, but that's actually a good sign that you're writing with your audience's needs in mind. Here are some examples:

- **Public speaking experience:** Delivered multimedia presentations to groups of 100+ weekly; developed strong ability to handle spontaneous Q&A while teaching college courses ranging from beginner to advanced level. (Notice that you don't need to name the courses or how many of them you taught.)
- **Project management:** Worked with team of ten writers to produce campus publication on weekly deadline. (Notice that you don't need to say what your title was or what the publication was.)
- **Leadership (or teamwork):** Led groups of high school students on summer backpacking trips in the Adirondack

Mountains. Worked with three other leaders to ensure safety of campers.

- **Computer skills:** Knowledge of [list software program names here]. (Note that you don't have to say how well you know each one—if you've done any work at all with the program, that's enough.)

One of the biggest disadvantages that academics face in writing résumés is that they've been trained to be scrupulously exact. Résumés require a different frame of mind. No, we're not suggesting that you should lie on your résumé. But as the previous examples show, standards of proof are quite different outside the academy. In fact, most people would say that academic standards are bizarrely specific.

For example, your CV would carefully detail whether you were a teaching assistant, a lecturer, or a faculty member, and you'd be sure to give the full title of every course that you've ever taught. But on your résumé, you should provide only a concise summary: "College-level instructor, taught economics courses ranging from beginner to advanced levels." Your classes should not be enumerated, but characterized. The details just don't matter much outside the academy.

When you describe summer jobs or part-time work, you also need to be careful you don't sell yourself short. "But I was just a lowly summer intern at a museum," you say. Well, we'd bet that you learned a great deal about how museums work and probably contributed more than your title would indicate. Your résumé should reflect the best of that experience, not what your W-2 says about you. Try to let go of the insecurities about "expertise" that academia fosters; take a kindly view of yourself, and you'll do a better job of presenting your true value and potential.

Reimagine Your Future

In order to write a persuasive résumé and cover letter, you're going to have to learn much more about your target audience. It's impossible to create a convincing argument without having a clear, specific thesis in mind. Think about those awful papers that English 101 students turn in with mind-bogglingly general theses like "Since the beginning of time, man has needed heroes." To a teacher who's trying to evaluate whether the student has understood *Wuthering Heights,* this paper doesn't look promising. Avoid that same pitfall in writing your résumé by knowing exactly whom you are trying to reach and what they want to hear from you.

The key is focusing on the challenges and obstacles each company faces. That's what you're looking for in this phase of your research. What do they need and how can you help? That means doing more than just reading their list of job openings. It means reading between the lines to find out as much as you can about a potential employer.

Maybe you have a notion that you'd like to work in publishing but don't know which part of the business or what kind of firm. Narrow your focus by asking your networking contacts, your career office staff, or anyone else you know about the differences between particular companies within an industry. Ask them to describe the differences in culture, approach, and priorities at these companies. Pick a few that interest you, and dig deeper to get an idea of how they work and where they are going. Do most people pay their dues by starting out as an administrative assistant? Or would you be better off trying to get your foot in the door as a copy editor? The more you know about how the place works, the easier it will be to write your résumé and cover letter.

If it sounds like we're asking you to invest an awful lot of time before even writing the first line of your résumé, that's exactly right. Not only does advance research make your résumé more effective, but it helps you figure out whether this firm is really where you want to spend forty hours of your week. It's a waste of your time to apply to a company you don't know anything about.

When Dina Venezky, a Ph.D. in geology, decided to leave academia, she started her company research by going to job fairs in Silicon Valley: "I really recommend trying out job fairs. Tell the recruiter about your background, your skills, and how you think you could help them. Get their business card, and then e-mail them the next day. Ask them specific questions in the e-mail so they have to answer you." Venezky also used e-mail newsgroups to find out about companies that interested her: "They were great for finding out what it's like to work there and what they look for in new employees. It's basically an information interview online."

Here are some other places to start your résumé research:

- **Company website:** Almost every company, nonprofit foundation, organization, or institution out there has a website. Start with your target organization's website to see how they define themselves and their problems. How are the company's divisions organized? How do they compare to their competition? If the annual report is available online, check out the president's message (or request an annual report via the public relations department.) Most websites also feature press releases that will give you a good idea of important recent events.
- **Company research** (*www.wetfeet.com*): You need to register as a member with Wetfeet, a job research site, to access some of their voluminous information about various companies. But your reward for forking over your name and e-mail address is free insight into hundreds of companies, including information on the recruiting process, interview style, key differentiating factors, and Q&A's with corporate recruiters.
- **Media:** You can learn a lot about the problems a company faces by reading press accounts of their ups and downs. Ask a reference librarian for help tracking media coverage of the company. Don't try to read every little blurb about the firm, but look for big articles about industry trends that may include the firm you want to track. You can also call the investor relations or public relations department of the company and ask for background information.

- **Your college's career services office:** The staff at the career services office are experts in finding information about jobs, careers, and companies. Make a list of the kind of information you need, and then make an appointment to tap into their knowledge.

Writing a Résumé: The First Draft

Once you've researched your target industries and companies, it's time to start thinking about a résumé format. Despite what some résumé books may tell you, there's no one magic formula guaranteed to land you a position. The two most common formats for organizing résumés are reverse chronological and skills-based. You may find that your best bet is a hybrid of the two. Ultimately, the format you use should be dictated by the job to which you're applying and the kind of experience you have to offer. We recommend that you try out both formats to see the advantages and disadvantages of each.

Reverse Chronological Résumé

The reverse chronological résumé is the one most people know best. List your experience from most recent to least recent. The trick here is to focus on the events that will interest the employer, without breaking the timeline or leaving any odd-looking gaps.

Advantages: This style is great for someone whose current job is in the field that they want to enter. The reader will identify you largely by the first entry on your résumé, so make sure it represents you as you want to be seen. This format also lets you choose between emphasizing either the companies you've worked for (**The World Bank,** summer intern and coffee gofer) or the positions you've held (**Statistician,** Some Tiny Little Company Unrelated to Your Major Interest).

Disadvantages: The reverse chronological format can trip you up pretty quickly if the string of experiences that you want to present doesn't work chronologically. Maybe you're adjunct teaching right now, but you want to apply for a job that's not related to teaching. Check out our sample résumés to see how other alumni handled this situation. The bottom line is that your résumé should answer questions, not raise them. If it looks funny to you, it'll look even more strange to an employer.

Skills-Based Résumé

If you've had little direct experience in the industry or field you hope to join, it may be easier to sell yourself by translating your past jobs into concrete skills rather than focusing on the jobs themselves. Your company research is crucial here. What skills are important to them? What are the company's priorities? Then you can map your experience onto their framework.

Advantages: A skills-based résumé is much more accommodating for people who've had unusual career paths (actually, that includes just about everybody). You can also grab an employer's attention more quickly if your résumé spells out exactly the skills they're looking for.

Disadvantages: Too much freedom can be a bad thing. Be careful to make your résumé "show, not tell." If you're presenting yourself as having public relations skills, you should be able to give evidence of some relevant experience that doesn't require too much interpretation on the reader's part. Also, many a grad student has added subheadings for research and writing skills to their CV and called it a résumé. Don't fall into that trap.

Remember that you probably have a more diverse set of skills than you realize. Clinging exclusively to your academic achievements may keep you from discovering your other assets. For example, Margit Dementi, a Ph.D. in comparative literature, had a difficult time removing her academic publications from her work history. She'd spent years laboring over these projects; it seemed unfair that they shouldn't be mentioned on her résumé. But since she was applying for management consulting jobs, they had to go. Once she condensed her academic achievements, she realized there was room on her résumé to highlight some of the skills she had acquired during her many years of working off and on at her family's photography studio in Richmond, Virginia.

She remembers that while working at the studio, she "discovered a stash of hundreds of old hand-colored window samples—beautiful pieces of work." Inspired, she set to work:

> I identified the portraits, researched our historical files, contacted the families, and placed an advertisement in the newspaper offering these photos for sale at an attractive price (just imagine a hand-painted picture of your wife or husband or mother—or grandfather—something that would cost hundreds or even thousands of dollars). We made a fair amount of money. These samples were simply gathering dust and would otherwise have been thrown away. They certainly would not have generated any income.

When incorporated into her résumé (and later described to employers during interviews), this informal experience showed how Dementi used creative problem-solving, research skills, and marketing savvy to increase the bottom line of a business.

A Few More Words of Advice

Experiment with career statements.

You might have seen résumés that have a "skill overview" or "career summary" statement at the top. They usually read something like "A manager with twelve years' experience seeking a challenging position in the hospitality industry." Should you try this approach? A good career statement can help you, but a bad one can hurt you, so you'll have to test-drive a few with your network of contacts in order to decide what works best for you (or if you need one at all).

The most effective career statements are concise, specific, and clearly focused. They should address the employer's needs (have we mentioned this before?) and clarify why you are the right person for the job. Try summarizing and emphasizing your relevant experience: Five years of experience in laboratory research? Six years of experience in student mentoring? Experienced researcher and writer with extensive knowledge of economics? If you don't have strong experience in the field you want to enter, you can at least highlight your interest and relevant skills here. See our sample résumés for ideas on how to use career statements wisely.

A word of caution: Avoid vague and long-winded career statements at all costs. Listing as your objective "Seeking challenging position in an environmentally friendly company where I can grow and succeed" will sink an otherwise strong résumé. While that sentence may indeed describe exactly what you're looking for in a job, the career statement is not the place to advertise your wish list.

Keep your résumé to one page.

How, you may ask, can you distill all your years of education, original research, teaching, conference papers, mentoring, and scholarship onto one page? This is the wrong question. Remember, focus on your prospective employer, not on yourself. Chances are that the hiring manager who receives your résumé will spend about thirty seconds reading it—which means they'll never get to the second page. So make it short and easy to scan.

A lot of items that belong on a CV are redundant on a résumé. This may hurt a little, but here's a list of what *not* to include on your résumé:

- the title of your dissertation (list your field of study instead)
- titles or descriptions of courses you've taught (summarize your experience in a short phrase: "three years teaching college-level biology")
- the awards you've won as either an undergrad or a grad student (except maybe one biggie)
- your advisers' names

- your references
- your M.A. date if you earned your Ph.D. at the same institution
- the conferences you've attended
- the articles or books you've published, unless directly relevant to the job you want

Use CAPITALIZATION, bold, *italics,* <u>underlining</u>, and white space.

Don't be afraid to highlight your strongest credentials with visual cues. Most of the CV's we've read (and sent out) have been pretty dry-looking documents—they list a candidate's education and dissertation at the top followed by a list of classes taught and articles published, all in tiny Times New Roman type. It's okay to make things a little more visually appealing outside the academy. This doesn't mean that you should use a script typeface and pink paper. It's just to say that you can be a little more creative with the aesthetics of your résumé.

Try some new vocabulary.

Every résumé needs some active verbs to make it powerful. If it seems like the only verbs that describe your academic experience are "wrote" and "researched," try using some of the following to describe the breadth of your experience:

Achieved	Coached	Developed
Analyzed	Collaborated	Evaluated
Applied	Communicated	Excelled
Arranged	Conducted	Explained
Assessed	Convinced	Explored
Assisted	Coordinated	Guided
Authored	Created	Identified
Balanced	Defined	Illustrated
Built	Described	Increased
Cataloged	Designed	Initiated

Introduced	Performed	Shaped
Invented	Presented	Solved
Led	Produced	Taught
Managed	Proved	Trained
Mentored	Recruited	Won
Negotiated	Researched	
Organized	Reviewed	

After You've Drafted a Résumé

Show it to your network.

It cost you some blood, sweat, and tears, but you've made a résumé. Now it's time to get it critiqued. It's crucial that you share your résumé with as many people in your network as possible. They'll be able to tell you what does and doesn't work, what kind of lingo you need to use, and how to present yourself in the best light. You should listen carefully to their advice and keep revising. It will take quite a few tries to come up with an effective résumé, and you'll have to make alternate versions for different kinds of jobs or industries. But the more you work on your résumé, the more you'll learn about the field and about how to position yourself within it.

Build your experience.

Maybe you've tried and tried to develop a good-looking résumé, but your experience just doesn't fit what you want to do. You can't change the past, so what are you supposed to do? Well, consider it a sign of what you need to do next: broaden your experience. If you're breaking into an entirely new field, talk with your network about what your résumé lacks and how you might get your feet wet. Should you get a part-time job, temp work, or volunteer work? Should you take a class? Should you try approaching your target company from a different perspective altogether? Can you do freelance or consulting work in the field? (If you skipped over chapter 3, now's a good time to go back to it.)

REAL-WORLD WRITING SAMPLES

It's common for employers in all kinds of fields to ask applicants to submit a writing sample either with a résumé or before an interview. Since you've poured your heart into your dissertation, you may be tempted to use it (or a related journal article) as evidence of your way with words. Don't do it. While your dissertation may be an example of your finest academic writing, it is absolutely not appropriate to use as a real-world writing sample.

Just as you had to learn the formalities of academic writing, you'll have to absorb the principles of post-academic writing in order to meet the employer's expectations. Most firms want to see a direct and concise style. (Don't hesitate to ask an employer what exactly they want to see in a writing sample, but don't be surprised if the answer is vague.) Your sample should be as short as possible: no longer than ten pages, but closer to five is better. A little personality or humor in the writing can catch the employer's eye, but strive for clarity above all else. Avoid academic jargon at all costs.

So where do you get experience in this kind of writing? If you're considering writing as a career, it's a great idea to write freelance articles for the local newspaper or the alumni magazine. One academic we met told us that he was preparing for a possible career change to journalism by writing occasional articles for *Runner's World* magazine. He was a serious long-distance runner, and he loved writing pieces on his favorite subject. You can try adapting this strategy to your own interests. Freelance writing rarely pays well, but knowing that you're creating a valuable portfolio can make the effort worthwhile.

But what if you need a writing sample right away? It's perfectly acceptable to improvise. You don't need to turn in published work. You could choose any format that you find comfortable: opinion piece, magazine article, narration of a personal experience. Your best bet, however, is to write about a topic related to the job you're seeking. You can use your customized writing sample as another opportunity to strengthen the case for hiring you.

Case Studies and Sample Résumés

In this section, you'll find four résumés created by people seeking their first full-time position outside academia. We've described the kind of jobs that each person was seeking so that you can see how they adapted their résumés to the employer's needs. We are grateful to all of these alumni for letting us use their real-life résumés (some identifying details have been changed) for educational purposes.

Case Study #1: Steve Sampson, A.B.D. Human Sciences: How to Write a Résumé with Little Post-Academic Experience

Steve Sampson was in his fourth year of a doctoral program in the human sciences at George Washington University when he decided that it was time to look for a career outside the academy. Although his research in early modern rhetoric continued to interest him, he was frustrated by low wages for adjuncts and the poor job prospects that lay ahead after he finished the program. When he and his wife found out they were expecting a baby, he made his decision to look for jobs outside the academy.

Sampson drafted several résumés before he came up with the version presented here. He found after sharing his first draft with some of his networking contacts that he needed to do some freelance writing on general interest topics to expand his experience. After completing a few assignments as a freelancer, he was able to produce a much stronger résumé.

Here's the ad Sampson answered:

A growing media company needs an experienced editor to develop copy about entertainment, child development, health, travel, and a variety of other topics. Web research experience a plus. Send résumé and clips.

Steven T. Sampson
3000 Madison Street
Arlington, VA 02232
(703) 888-8888
ssampson@grads.com

Objective: a career in publishing

Qualifications:

- Writing and editing skills developed through graduate education, professional freelancing, and experience teaching composition at George Washington University. Experience with a wide variety of styles and project types, from academic conference papers to editing memos, reports, business proposals, and training manuals.

- Researching skills honed through academic and professional research projects. Web researching skills developed through academic and freelance projects on subjects ranging from holiday meals to gastrointestinal disorders.

Education:

Ph.D. candidate, Human Sciences program, George Washington University
B.S., summa cum laude, English and Political Science, James Madison University

Work History:

1998–1999   **Adjunct Faculty Member,** George Washington University
- Designed and taught introductory composition course: developed syllabus, created lesson plans, supervised writing workshops.

1998–1999   **Researcher,** Thomas Nelson Company, *The Arden Shakespeare*
- Researched art and manuscript files at the Folger Shakespeare Library to identify materials for a pending online and multi-media edition of Shakespeare's work.

1997–1998   **Graduate Instructor,** George Washington University Writing Center
- Worked one-on-one with a variety of graduate and undergraduate students to improve their writing.

1994–1995   **Paralegal,** Sonnenschein, Nath & Rosenthal
- Researched factual documents for evidence in complex environmental, insurance, and government contract cases. Managed multiple cases on tight deadlines. Edited in-house paralegal training manual. Created electronic databases summarizing case files.

Sampson does a great job of breaking down his academic experience and showing the employer how it relates to his needs:

- The skills-based section at the top of the résumé under "Qualifications" allows Sampson to highlight the qualities that the employer seeks. A chronological format would have overemphasized his teaching experience.
- His career objective declares his interest in publishing, which is useful since his experience doesn't naturally translate into the field. His "Qualifications" section speaks directly to the ad's requirements. He highlights the range and variety of his experience as a writer and researcher. He also mentions web research experience, as the ad requested.
- When describing his qualifications, Sampson characterizes his experience broadly rather than listing every detail of what he did. He gives an overview and then lists specific examples to convey variety: "subjects ranging from holiday meals to gastrointestinal disorders."
- The education section is condensed and simple. In earlier versions, he had detailed his credentials at length, listing his dissertation topic, advisers, etc.
- Sampson includes his teaching experience under "work history." The work history serves to answer the question raised by the skills-based section of the résumé: What has he been doing for the past few years? To that end, he has put the dates of employment first, instead of the job titles.

Case Study #2: Karen Rignall, A.B.D. Anthropology: How to Make Part-Time Work Add Up to Full-Time Experience

Karen Rignall decided to leave her anthropology Ph.D. program at the University of Michigan shortly after finishing her general exams. She had been planning to do her fieldwork in Morocco but decided that she needed to find a different way to pursue her love of North African and Middle Eastern cultures.

KAREN EUGENIE RIGNALL

300 Green Ave., Apt. 3
Brooklyn, New York 11238
(718) 555-5555

PROFESSIONAL EXPERIENCE

Arab Community Center for Economic and Social Services (ACCESS), Dearborn, MI
Program Assistant   1996–1998
- Designed program plan and assisted in fund-raising and initial start-up for an innovative job-placement service to support the workforce development initiatives currently being undertaken at ACCESS
- Successfully wrote $300,000 grant to fund construction of a new $3.8 million ACCESS multiservice center
- Developed program plans and successfully wrote grants for projects involving employment generation, training, and immigration advocacy and services

Catholic Relief Services, Rabat, Morocco
Training Officer/Program Assistant   1992–1993
- Developed and wrote $3 million proposal for a micro-credit project that was subsequently approved by the U.S. Agency for International Development
- Assisted management of initiative to provide financial support and training to Moroccan development associations
- Developed, oversaw, and evaluated community development projects with Moroccan counterparts
- Prepared and delivered training in project management for grant recipients

United States Agency for International Development, Dakar, Senegal
Researcher/Program Assistant   1992
- Conducted field study on wholesale rice marketing in Senegal
- Developed recommendations for USAID agricultural programs on the basis of this study

CARE Egypt, Cairo, Egypt
Researcher   1991
- Researched and wrote analysis of poverty alleviation efforts and the Egyptian economic situation for use in the CARE multiyear planning document
- Conducted informal evaluation of micro-credit project implemented in four provinces

Department of Anthropology, University of Michigan, Ann Arbor
Graduate Student Instructor   1997–1998
- Taught courses on cross-cultural understanding

EDUCATION

M.A., University of Michigan–Ann Arbor
Field: Middle East History (forthcoming, 1998)
M.P.A., Woodrow Wilson School for Public and International Affairs, Princeton University
Field: International Development Studies (1994)
B.A., Princeton University
Field: International Development/Near Eastern Studies (1992)

LANGUAGE SKILLS
French (fluent), Arabic (fluent), Spanish (highly proficient)

Her short-term goal was to find work related to these interests that would sustain her while she learned how to build her own Moroccan import business. The résumé she shared with us helped her land a fund-raising job at an international women's foundation.

Rignall highlights part-time jobs she held during graduate school, rather than her academic experience, to create a highly persuasive résumé. Although the part-time jobs were fairly low-level experience, she worked for well-known groups whose missions were relevant to her audience. Let's analyze how she chose to present herself for this fund-raising job:

- Rignall uses a chronological format, but deemphasizes the dates of each position by listing them at the end of each line. Instead of trying to create a seamless chronology, she simply lists the years of each experience.
- Although teaching is her most recent position, she lists it at the end, which disrupts the chronology. But since teaching is not particularly relevant to this position, putting it last completes her work history without distracting the employer from the more important items listed above.
- Rignall has worked for several interesting overseas organizations, so she lists the names of the groups ahead of her job title. Putting the locations (Dakar, Senegal) in bold type helps the reader pick up quickly that she has extensive experience living and working abroad.
- Her descriptions of each job place her work in the context of larger projects, rather than limiting herself to the boundaries of her job titles. For example, she lists the dollar amounts of the grants she won for the agencies and describes herself as assisting with major initiatives. Rignall also describes several specific projects that she designed and carried out, which shows that she can initiate and follow through on new ideas.
- In describing her teaching experience, Rignall lists only the general topic of the classes she taught.
- Under "Education," Rignall chooses to emphasize her fields of study rather than the degrees awarded. Because her fields

show long-standing interest and experience, they are a good choice for her limited space.

Case Study #3: Dina Venezky, Ph.D. Geology: How to Give Them What They Want

Dina Venezky entered the Silicon Valley job market armed with plenty of knowledge about how different companies worked and what they wanted to see in job candidates. Her husband, a physics Ph.D., had been recruited by Sun Microsystems, but she had to work a little harder to help employers see her value.

Venezky went to several job fairs to find out who was hiring and to make contacts. She joined e-mail discussion groups to get the inside scoop on her target companies. Once Venezky decided to apply to a technology consulting company, she drew up a résumé that reflected the results of her research. It's also important to note that all of the experience on her résumé was gained during grad school:

- Venezky uses a skills-based résumé so she can match her experience to the qualities she knows the employer wants. She organizes the items in each category according to their relevance, instead of their chronology.
- Venezky knows that physicists are in high demand, so she emphasizes her experience in geophysics instead of just listing geology as her field of study. This small step goes a long way to keeping an employer's attention while scanning her résumé. She also highlights her computer experience in a separate section to draw attention to her extensive technical skills, which might not be otherwise expected from a geology Ph.D.
- Venezky includes some unusual experiences that make reading her résumé more interesting. The mention of her minor in studio art, her experience leading wilderness trips, and her "Fruit-a-Burst Girl" role let the reader know that she's creative and innovative.

Dina Y. Venezky, Ph.D.

123 Lois Lane, Apt. C, Metropolis, ME 12345 555-555-5555
dyvz@gradstudent.edu   http://gradstudent.edu/dina

EDUCATION

Brown University, Providence, RI, Ph.D. Geology, concentration in geophysics, 1997
Smith College, Northampton, M.A., A.B. Geology, concentration in studio art, 1992

LEADERSHIP

Project Manager, Solar System Exploration Pilot Student Workshop, Jet Propulsion Laboratory, 1996
Oversaw all aspects of Venus Aerobot mission from choosing science objectives and instruments, to leading the group, to managing costs ($150 M) and environmental constraints. Designed presentation for NASA review panel.

Liaison for the Center for Advancement of College Teaching, 1995–1996
Designed a workshop for all science teaching assistants to introduce them to practices at Brown.

National Outdoor Leadership School, Semester in the Rocky Mountains, Fall 1990
Led groups in wilderness backpacking, caving, desert backpacking, and winter telemarking.

COMPUTING AND MULTIMEDIA

Webmaster, Brown University Geology WWW Server, 1993
Designed and developed first public United States Geology Department Web server. Experience in Perl, Fortran and C. Familiar with Unix, Mac OS, LaTeX, HTML, JAVA and applications.

TEACHING

President's Award for Excellence, Brown University, 1995
Instructor for the Brown Learning Community, 1995–1996
Taught classes to students of all ages and their parents about volcanoes, rocks and minerals, mission design, and using the World Wide Web to learn more about science.
Teaching Assistant, Brown University, 1992–1994
Taught geochemistry and physical geology.

EXTRACURRICULAR

Volunteer at the X-Games. Created and filled the role of FRUIT-A-BURST girl.
Volunteer at Wind Cave National Park, South Dakota
On Eagles' Wings Scientist Presenter, Lindbergh Foundation

- Under "Teaching," Venezky lists several items that highlight her versatility as a teacher. Teaching awards are good résumé material, especially for consulting companies, which will want to know if she can communicate with a variety of audiences.

Case Study #4: Josh Fost, Ph.D. Neurobiology: How to Hit the Highlights

Josh Fost became an expert on the brain of the sea slug during grad school. At first glance, this knowledge may not seem terribly marketable. But while studying slug brains, Fost developed sophisticated computer models to track the results of his experiments. (They involved a record turntable, a beaker full of slugs, and a desk lamp . . . don't ask.) Fost knew that he had the computer skills to be a technical consultant. He also knew that he had the personality to do well in the field because he had worked for himself helping people purchase and set up home computers.

The key to Fost's résumé is the overview. He tells the employer most of what they want to know about his technical capabilities in the first few lines of his résumé. All that's left is to show that he has the project management and people skills to handle the job:

- Fost uses a chronological format because his skills are clearcut and well defined. Since the overview establishes his concrete skills immediately, it's okay that his first entry under work experience is slightly out of the field.
- Fost describes his degree as "computational neuroscience," to emphasize the connection between his degree and the job.
- Stating exactly what position he seeks and the amount of travel he'd like to do helps answer the employer's major questions right away. It also shows that Fost has done his research: consulting jobs involve an enormous amount of travel.

Josh W. Fost, Ph.D.

1 Summer St.   (555) 555-1313

Somerville, MA 02143   fost@grad.com

OVERVIEW

- 9 years C/C++ development (Unix, Win95/NT, Mac OS)
- Ph.D. in computational neuroscience, strong quantitative modeling and statistical skills
- Seeking project management position, 30% travel

EXPERIENCE

1996–1998   **Postdoctoral fellow, Brandeis University**
- Translated nonquantitative biological problems into quantitative models.
- Developed C++ applications and user interfaces to test models.
- Designed computational models of active filters in neurons; measures of salience in time-series.

1996–1998   **Computer consultant, freelance**
- Helped nontechnical home users with system purchases and troubleshooting.
- Web design and development (DHTML, CSS, JavaScript).
- Systems administration (Unix, Win95/NT): 20-machine campus LAN.

1991–1996   **Graduate student, Princeton University**
- Computer modeling of biophysical mechanism of learning.
- Analysis of feedback and gain control in biological neural network.
- Research on stochastic resonance, role of noise in neural nets.

1991   **Research fellow, Naval Ocean Systems Center**
- Developed models of mammalian visual system for use in undersea vehicle.
- Researched flocking and swarming algorithms.

EDUCATION

1996   Ph.D. Computational neuroscience (neurobiology), Princeton University

1991   A.B. Neuroscience, philosophy, Bowdoin College

OTHER ACTIVITIES

- Cofounder and manager of college café, 1988–1991
- Interests: drawing, hiking, carpentry, poetry, juggling

- In his job descriptions, Fost emphasizes the analytical and technical skills that will translate into consulting work, rather than the biological knowledge involved.
- His freelance work was pretty informal, but it's fair game for this résumé. Whether he made a lot of money or a little, it's valuable and relevant experience to this employer.

Cover Letters That Will Get You Hired

Now that you've spent an enormous amount of time polishing your résumé, you might be tempted to dash off a cover letter in no time flat. Resist the temptation. The cover letter will be the first thing that your prospective employer sees and can absolutely determine whether you get an interview.

There are entire books devoted to the art of writing the perfect cover letter. We've adopted a slightly heretical approach, so you may want to check out some of those other books for more detail on the subject. Our wisdom boils down to one sentence: Keep it short and simple. You'll keep yourself out of trouble, and the employer will thank you for not wasting his or her time.

Most cover letters for academic appointments devote the better part of two single-spaced pages to explaining a dissertation topic, a philosophy of teaching, and so on. Cover letters for post-academic jobs, however, should be less than a page and should not mention your dissertation. Instead, highlight one or two key pieces of experience that show you're qualified for the job.

The goal of your cover letter should be to convey your enthusiasm for a particular job and give your best explanation of why you are well-suited for the position. As with the résumé, your focus should be on why you can do the job, not your life story. Don't talk about why you're thinking of leaving academia or how conflicted you are about the decision. Instead, say what interests you about the job and what experience makes you qualified to fill it.

Here's a basic outline to follow:

- **First paragraph:** Introduce yourself and express your interest in the job.
- **Second paragraph:** Highlight one or two particularly relevant pieces of experience.
- **Third paragraph:** Close by saying that you'll follow up with a phone call within a week.

As you develop your cover letter, **keep your language simple and direct.** Write in a style that feels natural to you. Imagine that you're speaking on the phone to someone you respect. Try to sound confident and clear, not stilted. Would you use phrases like "Thank you in advance for your anticipated cooperation" or "Please find my résumé enclosed for your perusal"? Substituting language such as "Thank you for your time" or "My résumé is enclosed for your review" will do just fine.

Attempting to sound somewhat friendly (or at least human) is a good goal, **but don't go overboard with humor or informality.** Another extreme to avoid is obsequiousness. Employers are not impressed when you try to flatter them about their "exciting opportunity at a remarkable company." Use specific examples to explain why you are excited about working for this firm, and avoid empty compliments.

If at all possible, **send your letter to a human being rather than "to whom it may concern."** Search the company website or call the main number to ask who the hiring manager for a particular position is and address your letter accordingly. If you have a personal contact, by all means mention it. Even if you have only the slightest connection with the recipient of your letter, highlight it: "I really enjoyed hearing you speak at the recent University of Maryland Graduate Career Forum. Your description of the varied tasks required of Program Associate convinced me that I would be well-suited for the position."

Finally, proofread. Then proofread again. Get someone else to proofread for you. Then proofread again. Wait twenty-four hours and proofread again. Nothing will send your materials to the trash can faster than typographical errors.

Here is a sample letter to get you started:

June 20, 2005

Ms. Sarah Barton
Editor
National Geographic
1000 Duke Street
Washington, DC 20000

Dear Ms. Barton,

Kate Jackson suggested that I contact you about the position you have open for a copy editor. I've been interested in working for *National Geographic* ever since I traveled solo around Africa after completing my Ph.D. in French at Boston University. Enclosed along with my résumé is a piece that I wrote for *Tigers Today* about my visit to a wildlife preserve for retired circus animals in Tanzania, which was one of the highlights of my trip.

I understand from Kate that you're looking for someone who speaks French, has traveled in Africa, and knows AP style. It appears that I fit the bill, and I'm excited at the prospect of working for a magazine I've subscribed to since I was a child. I look forward to talking with you further about this position.

Sincerely,
Julie Christie

This letter, while brief, begins with the name of a personal contact, includes a relevant interest, refers to a writing sample, and responds directly to the employer's needs (French and AP style). While every cover letter is unique, strive for a clear, conversational approach that clarifies your skills and illustrates how they match up with the job you seek.

Applying for jobs can be horribly nerve-racking. We've outlined the steps as if it's a simple 1-2-3 process, but we know that it just isn't that easy. While you're going through this process, seek out a buddy who can share the stress with you. Proofread each other's letters, cheer each other's successes, and boo each other's rejections. Every job hunter needs a friend.

....

POST-ACADEMIC PROFILE:
BRYAN GARMAN, PREP SCHOOL HEADMASTER,
PH.D. IN AMERICAN STUDIES

Bryan Garman became headmaster of Wilmington Friends School in Delaware after teaching history at Sidwell Friends School, a prestigious prep school in Washington, D.C., for many years. At Sidwell six of the nine teachers in his department had Ph.D.'s. He hadn't planned on going into high school teaching, but he realized as he was finishing his dissertation that it would allow him and his wife to live wherever they chose.

Garman had experience working with younger students from teaching gifted middle school kids in a summer program. This kind of practice is important for testing your love of teaching, he advises, and for proving to hiring committees that you really do want to teach younger kids.

As you would expect, his students are less mature than college students. They require him to be more entertaining during lectures, and he must monitor whether they are paying attention and taking notes during class. But, he says, "they're often as smart as college freshmen." He also likes the opportunity to "educate the whole student" as these teenagers develop emotionally. Since Sidwell, like many prep schools, requires its teachers to supervise extracurricular activities, he also has a more rounded perspective on his students from seeing them on the tennis courts and in school plays. He gradually took on more administrative work, which made him ideally suited for a headmaster position when one opened up at Wilmington Friends.

While Garman does sometimes miss the intellectual atmosphere of graduate school, he has "excellent colleagues and can make time to pursue academic writing on the side." His book on working-class heroes from Walt Whitman to Bruce Springsteen was published by an academic press.

For grad students applying to high school teaching jobs, Garman recommends revising your résumé to emphasize your love of teaching rather than your scholarship. Minimizing your use of academic jargon is also a good idea, he adds. Hiring committees also like to see evidence of a long-standing interest in teaching younger students, so relevant experience or a customized letter of recommendation can be a great asset as well.

5 Sweaty Palms, Warm Heart

How to Turn an Interview into a Job

"Nothing that you've learned about how to get jobs in the academy will help you find a job in the real world," says Carol Barash, a former professor of eighteenth-century literature at Rutgers who now runs her own advertising and strategic marketing firm. She's quick to add that the skills she acquired as a graduate student and professor have been essential to her success in the business world but that she needed to unlearn the lessons of the academic job-hunting process before searching for a job in business. "The academic search is so passive. I mean, in what other career search in the world are you supposed to send out a bunch of résumés and just wait for the phone to ring?"

If you've been trained to conduct an academic job search, you may think of the job interview as the most passive stage of the process. You just sit there while the interviewer asks you questions about your strengths and weaknesses, your greatest accomplishment, and your five-year plan, right? Wrong. When you're applying for jobs outside the academy, the interview is your chance to show that you can do the job. Let's restate that: The goal of the interview is to *prove* that you can do the job. You need to lower the risk of hiring you. Companies lose money on new employees at first because they have to train them, so they want to make sure they choose well. Remember in chapter 3 how we talked about the importance of getting some small amount of relevant experience to give yourself the benefit of the doubt, beyond your Ph.D. qualifications? It's the same principle in the interview process—you need to show that you're a safe bet.

Of course, the interview is also the time for you to decide whether you want to work for this company. While it's flattering to be invited for a "real world" interview after years in graduate school, don't make the mistake of thinking that you'll be lucky to have any job they offer. As one happily placed alum told us, "If I did it all over again, I'd remember that I'm supposed to be interviewing them as much as they are interviewing me." You may be in for an unpleasant surprise down the road if you rush to accept a job without thinking about whether you see yourself being happy and successful in the new environment.

As in writing a résumé, your research skills can help you in preparing for an interview. The more you know about a company, the more comfortable you'll be and the more smoothly your interview will go. Spend time reading the company's website and catching up on media coverage about the organization and issues relevant to its mission. If you're interviewing with the World Wildlife Fund, for example, look into other environmental groups with similar missions and form some ideas about what makes one different from another. It's amazing how few people do this kind of preparation for an interview, but it's key to your success. You should also continue to network with people who work in the same general field so that you can have an informed conversation with your interviewer.

Academics can also rely on their teaching skills to help an interviewer see their value. We're not suggesting that you should patronize your interviewer. A good teacher is confident and knowledgeable, but also interested in what others have to say. Geoff Davis, a Ph.D. in mathematics and a former professor at Dartmouth, found his teaching skills invaluable in landing a position at Microsoft. "One of the standard things in Microsoft interviews is that they send you to the board to solve problems, usually some kind of brain-teaser. The idea is to see how people think on their feet, and for most of their recruits, it's an unnerving and difficult situation. After teaching for four years, though, it was pretty easy for me. Put a piece of chalk in my hand and it's my show!"

How to Land a Job Interview

Davis was one of the incredibly fortunate few who were actually recruited by Microsoft. A Microsoft manager who was looking for a mathematician with good computer skills got his name from a mutual friend. "After chatting on the phone, he suggested I come by for an interview in a few days," Davis recalls. Although he was very happy as a professor at Dartmouth, he "decided to go, mostly out of curiosity, and also because it was kind of flattering to be flown across the country on two days' notice."

Most of us, however, probably won't be that lucky. Don't wait around for the phone to ring. Make your own luck. After you've sent out some résumés, use these strategies to turn your résumé into an interview.

Remember that just because there are no positions advertised doesn't mean there are no positions available.
Spending several years reading the job listings in the *Chronicle of Higher Education* or the official bulletin of your professional organization may be the worst training possible for a post-academic career search—it's too passive. While academic departments may wait years for approval to hire a new tenure-track professor, companies simply cannot afford to move that slowly. If a manager can demonstrate a clear need, he or she can usually get the go-ahead to make a hire. So don't wait around for a classified ad to appear before trying to network.

Cultivate relationships.
"Everyone says that 'networking' is key, and, sad to say, it's trite but true. All of my job interviews have come about because of someone I knew, not because my résumé or cover letter was in-

credibly impressive," advises Jerry Tyson, a former English professor at the University of Maryland who now works as an editor for the National Environmental Trust. This is actually great news for academic career-changers (especially those of you who feel frustrated after slogging through the last chapter on building a résumé). Don't dwell on the fact that you don't have six years of experience in marketing; you may be able to land a job interview by cultivating good relationships with some of your favorite contacts. Employers hire people, not résumés.

And don't imagine that the need to network ends once you've landed the interview or even the job. Once he took the job at Microsoft, Geoff Davis "made a point of introducing myself to people in other groups who were doing things I thought were interesting." When Davis's group was "reorganized out of existence," he was able to move easily into the Signal Processing Group at Microsoft Research because he had taken the time to build a network.

Before the Interview

So you've checked your voice mail fifteen times a day for two weeks and finally gotten that call you wanted: the company of your dreams wants you to come in for an interview. Fantastic! What do you do first? Call back the person who arranged the interview with you and ask everything you forgot to ask before: Who will I be meeting? How long will the interviews last? Is there a particular interview format they like to use, such as case-method questions? Hands-on trials? Written test? Is the office dress code business casual? Will you be going to lunch? These questions will let you know what to expect and reduce your anxiety. But these questions are only the beginning.

Make calls to your industry and company contacts and ask specific questions in order to prepare for the interview.

Let them know you are interviewing and that you want to find out more about specific issues the company faces. Be careful not

WHILE YOU'RE WAITING FOR AN INTERVIEW

Okay, so you've called all the hiring managers on your list and networked like crazy. What do you do while waiting for your interviews? Take the time to continue your research. It will help you relax and make you a better-prepared candidate. Try these strategies:

- **Test-drive their product.** Mark Johnson, an English Ph.D., used his personal experience balancing his budget with Quicken software to win a job at Intuit. He sought out the job because he liked the product, but he got the job because he could talk intelligently about how it was used. This level of involvement may be superficial, but it would look even worse if you were ignorant of it.
- **Follow up on media coverage.** Read about the industry and the specific company. Know what the trends are. Keep an eye out in newspapers and trade magazines for stories about the company; look up articles on big events in their past. For example, if the firm was taken over by a bigger company a few years ago, being able to talk to an interviewer about it intelligently will show you to your best advantage.
- **Evaluate the company.** Surf their website, watch their TV programs, answer their survey, use their soap, read their magazine. Whatever the company does, try out the product and make notes about the experience. The Motley Fool website likes candidates who have participated on their message boards, for example. The Discovery Channel asks candidates what their favorite Discovery show is and whether they have ideas for additional programming. Be prepared to ask informed questions and offer ideas.

to put anyone in an awkward situation. Your focus should be on the job, not on the personality of your interviewer or the odds of your being hired. Ask questions based on your research about the company and about what they need in an employee. You should already know what the firm's priorities are from your original research. Now take it step further and test out your perspective on the situation with a trusted contact.

Practice your two-minute introduction.
You need to be able to give a good two-minute introduction summarizing who you are and what you can do. While the two-minute pitch is also important in networking, in this case you're preparing for the interviewer who was unceremoniously pulled from his or her desk, dragged into the conference room, and handed your résumé. It happens all the time. In most offices, only one of the five or so people who may interview you has actually read your résumé in advance. Be prepared to make it easy for the people who are starting cold. Don't assume they know what you just told someone else. You need to supply these people with the rationale they'll need when someone asks them, "So, should we hire him/her?" Your two-minute pitch serves this important purpose by explaining who you are and how you'll fit into the company.

Prepare for standard kinds of interview questions.
Standard human resources screening questions include: What's your greatest strength? Worst fault? Do you prefer to work in a team or by yourself? How do you handle disappointment? Where do you see yourself in five years? Most career books have long lists of these questions and examples of good and bad answers. Don't worry too much about them, though. There are three points to remember about any interview question:

1. Always speak positively about yourself.
2. Use specific examples to make a point.
3. Try to turn the question toward the requirements of the job, rather than getting tangled up in an analysis of your personality.

For example, if you know that the job requires keeping a team project on schedule, you can say, "I'm a deadline-driven person, so I sometimes get frustrated by procrastinators. But I know that everyone has their own strengths and weaknesses to contribute. Here's an example: I collaborated on an article with a colleague who was terrible about meeting deadlines. But she was very creative and full of good ideas, so we each gave a little, and together we produced a top-notch article. It was a great experience, and from what I understand, that kind of teamwork is important in this job too."

Whatever you do, try to keep your answers relatively brief and concise. Richard Bolles—the author of *What Color Is Your Parachute?*—has found that the ideal response time to interview questions can be anywhere from twenty seconds to two minutes. Those of us used to writing 300-page dissertations that answer larger questions may have trouble confining ourselves to this limit, but concentrate on keeping it simple. Allow for give-and-take, with room for follow-up questions to elicit more detail as needed.

Try to find out ahead of time what types of questions you'll be asked.

Some industries like to move beyond standard interview questions to more surprising methods, like problem-solving exercises, employment tests, or case-management questions. Use your contacts to try to figure out in advance what kinds of things you'll be asked. (You may even want to set up a mock interview with a kindly contact.) Candidates for consulting jobs just might not be able to get away from questions like "How many Ping-Pong balls would it take to fill an airplane?" or "Why are manhole covers round?"

Some interviewers may spring completely off-the-wall questions on you. Jeff Bezos, founder of Amazon.com, likes to ask potential employees, "How would you design a car for deaf people?" Case-management techniques can help here too, but practicing how to stay calm and work out reasonable answers on the spot is probably the best approach. These kinds of questions usually don't have right or wrong answers. What the employers wants to see is how you analyze problems, how you work under pressure, and whether you can relate your answers to the job at hand.

Your graduate training gives you both an advantage and a disadvantage in these case-management/off-the-wall situations.

On the one hand, you're well-prepared to answer the question: you've been taught to get to the heart of a problem, so draw on that skill and do your best. On the other hand, your graduate training may make you too cautious. This isn't academia; you can't go research the problem for six months before you give an answer. Don't worry that you don't know anything about car design or maybe even about deaf people—just make your best guess based on what you know about the company.

Make your list of questions.

One Ph.D. told us that he approached his post-academic interviews as "anthropological expeditions into a strange new culture." Prepare for your fieldwork with a long list of questions because (1) there's a lot you need to know; (2) the interviewer's answers will help you answer their questions; and (3) it will help you relax. Don't hesitate to be curious about the company and how it works.

Here are some sample questions:

- What are the biggest challenges you face in your position?
- What are some ways you address those challenges?
- How could the person you hire help solve these problems?
- What's the biggest short-term challenge for this company as a whole?
- What are the long-range challenges for the company?

(Show your knowledge of the company in your response to whatever they say. These questions will help you start off a discussion about what needs to be done and how you can help, which is exactly the tone you want your interview to take.)

- What would a typical day/week be like in this job? How much time can I expect to spend on meetings/travel/independent work each week?
- What types of personalities do well in this kind of job? What are the trademarks of people who are successful here?
- Who would I report to? Who does that person report to?

- What happened to the last person in this job? What's the usual career trajectory from here?
- What's the typical background for people I'd be working with?
- What's your hiring philosophy? Are there certain qualities that are non-negotiable, that a candidate must have?

These questions are designed to help you evaluate whether or not you want the job. Listen carefully to the responses, and think about whether you want to work in this environment.

An important note: Remember that you should not discuss salary until you have a written job offer in hand. If an interviewer asks you about your salary requirements or history, do not respond with specific numbers. No matter how much they persist that they need a dollar figure, simply reassure them in a warm and friendly tone: "I'm very interested in working here, but I'm just not comfortable discussing salary without a written offer. I'm sure we'll be able to work out a salary that's agreeable to both of us when the time comes."

During the Interview

Here you are in your best (read: only) suit, sitting alone in a huge conference room with a cup of lukewarm coffee, waiting for your first inquisitor. The person enters, shakes your hand, and you sit down again, wiping your sweaty palm on your knee. How do you stay calm? Nick Corcodilos has some great advice on this subject: "Start your meeting by making the interviewer talk. Most interviewers allow time at the start of an interview for idle chat. They're trying to relax you. Take advantage of this. Don't wait for the employer to ask the first question."

An easy way to start is by asking your interviewer how long they've been with the company and what s/he does. Getting your interviewer to talk about his or her role will give you a chance to relax as well as offering some insights that can help shape your answers later in the interview. It's also never a bad idea to let someone talk about themselves. Whatever you do, be confident and be clear—even if you're bluffing. Woody Allen once said that 90 percent of life is just showing up. We'd say that 90 percent of job hunting is showing up and looking confident. For an employer to understand the enormous value that your academic training has to offer, you must first be convinced of it yourself. It's up to you to persuade the employer that you're a good bet; you're not presenting yourself in the hope that they will find you worthy of any old position in the company. You have tangible skills and experience to offer; you can make this employer's life easier if s/he hires you.

Teach Someone How to Read Your Résumé

Here's where all those years of teaching undergraduate sections of Spanish 101 or Intro to Art History will come in handy. We mentioned earlier that some of your interviewers are likely to have been yanked from their desks only moments before meeting you. They've just been handed your résumé on the way down the hall, and they never got to see that cover letter you worked so hard to get just right. In most cases, these interviewers are people who won't be working directly with you (so they're not too engaged in the whole process), but the hiring manager is going to ask their opinion of your value. It can be a tough audience. But you can handle these kinds of interviewers skillfully if you realize in advance that they will probably be relying heavily on your résumé to guide their questions. So if you practice talking about the items on your résumé in a way that highlights the relevant points, you can teach them to see you as a person with valuable skills and experience.

Here's an example:

Interviewer, glancing at your résumé: "Hmmm . . . so what's the Jubilee Theater Group?" (What s/he means is: "What on earth does that have to do with this job?")

Weak answer: "Well, they put on lots of productions on campus; they do kind of avant-garde stuff compared to the more traditional theater groups. Last year they did a version of *West Side Story* set in Nazi Germany that was just amazing."

Strong answer: "It's a campus theater group—I was stage manager for three years. I was responsible for coordinating all of the technical elements of our shows, ensuring that all of the equipment worked correctly and that we hit all of the technical cues. It was a great experience and taught me a lot about project management and grace under pressure."

Be prepared to speak specifically about how each item on your résumé relates to a skill or an experience that will be valuable to the person sitting in front of you. And then try to turn the conversation back to understanding and addressing the company's challenges and what qualities they need in the person they hire for this job.

Overcoming Stereotypes about Ph.D.'s

While a Ph.D. on your résumé can get you noticed by a potential employer, it can also lead an interviewer to pass judgment on you and your skills based on stereotypes about eggheaded professors. Jennifer Scott knows all about the stereotypes because she's a former graduate student in early modern history at Columbia. One of the duties in her role as a senior producer/content manager for Morningside Ventures, Columbia University's for-profit digital media company, is to recruit and interview new employees. Here are a few of her tips for handling negative perceptions of Ph.D.'s:

Academics aren't sufficiently focused on producing results.
Ph.D.'s have a reputation for "belaboring a point to its logical (or illogical) conclusion," Scott says. We're taught to argue, criticize, deconstruct, and to "debate for the sake of debate."

What she would like to see academics do in interview situations is "to show evidence of moving forward," show that they can produce results rather than simply discuss a problem. For example, one philosopher we interviewed was frustrated that his department paid little attention to training grad students to teach. Rather than rage against the system, he took action by organizing a semester-long teaching workshop for new graduate assistants. Not only did he improve the state of pedagogy in his department; he also came up with a good interview story that gives clear evidence of his ability to get things done.

Academics can't work in teams.
Pursuing a Ph.D. is a supremely solitary pursuit. Sure, you may do some teaching, but writing your dissertation requires that you spend countless hours working alone in libraries and archives. Be prepared to give "some evidence that you can work with others," advises Scott. Volunteer work and hobbies are fair game here.

Academics aren't risk-takers.
"Academic work is very measured," Scott says. "You're used to doing all the research before you say anything. In this world [the Internet industry], you have to get comfortable moving ahead with much less information."

Most of the questions you'll be asked in interviews don't have wrong answers. Many times the interviewer just wants to see how you think and react to new information. Interviewers expect you to have researched the organization and understand its mission, but they don't expect you to be an expert. So go ahead, hazard a guess. In many businesses it's better to be a little wrong than to be so cautious that you can't act.

You shouldn't worry too much about these stereotypes, for they are easily overcome with evidence of your success in non-academic endeavors. Ultimately, your chances as a Ph.D. of being hired are as good, or better, than anyone else's. Also, these issues are only raised in connection to a Ph.D.'s first post-academic job—once you've got some experience working outside academia, no one will bother you with these kinds of questions again.

What to Say about Graduate School

You'll learn a lot about your interviewer from how they react to the graduate education listed on your résumé. Don't assume that one person's reaction will hold true for the rest of the company. Alumni have reported encountering these reactions:

- "Why do I need someone with all that education?"
- "I thought about going to grad school, but I didn't get in."
- "Why did it take so long for you to finish?" Or "Why didn't you finish?"
- "Gosh, you must be really smart." Or "I'd better watch my grammar."
- "Why would you want to work here?"
- "My brother-in-law has a Ph.D.—I never understood why anyone would go to all that trouble."
- "Are you just killing time until next year? Would you go back to academia if a job opened up?"

Academic credentials impress many people. But they can also make some folks hostile or suspicious. Be prepared to make graceful, concise, and upbeat comments about your grad school experience. Maybe your feelings are still a little raw; maybe you plan to go on the market again next year. Don't talk about that during the interview. Just speak about the overall experience as a challenge that you met successfully, and one in which you learned a great many skills that you'd like to apply in a new context. You've become an expert in one field—there's no reason why you can't become just as proficient in another. So you left in the middle of your program? That's nothing to be ashamed of. More than 99 percent of the population has never been enrolled in a doctoral program, so they should have no trouble understanding why you left.

Don't feel that you have to spill all the gory details; your interviewer is far less interested in this topic than you think s/he is. Be concise and selective in your response. It's extremely common for alums who haven't yet made peace with their decision to talk nonstop for fifteen minutes about departmental politics when asked why they want to leave academia. Unfortunately, these kinds of angst-ridden responses are a sure way to knock yourself out of the running for any job.

Weak Answers:
- "I've been on the market five times, and I've been an adjunct for three years. I'm still working on turning my dissertation into a book, but I have to find something else for now."
- "I've loved my dissertation topic, but it just wasn't fashionable enough for the job market. There's a lot of politics around what kind of positions are filled in modern language departments these days. Because I wasn't interested in literary theory, my topic just didn't appeal to hiring committees, so I only got a few on-campus interviews."
- "Well, I don't really want to leave academia, but I can't afford to buy a house on the money I make as an adjunct and we're about to have another kid."

Strong Answers:
Better answers to these questions include references to the big financial sacrifices and the narrowness of academia. These are elements that anyone can understand, and citing them will shield you from slipping into a long, painful, and overly personal narrative.

- "Grad school was a great experience, but it just wasn't making any financial sense for me in the long term. I've decided to take the next step and bring my love of science and my lab research skills to industry."
- "I loved teaching, but academia's a small, narrow world. I felt there just had to be better opportunities out there for me, other ways to use my skills. I've been writing magazine articles on the side for years just because I enjoy it, so I finally decided to take the plunge and devote myself to journalism full-time."

Should You Mention That You Might Go on the Market Again?

In short, no. It would be foolish for any employer to hire someone who says that she plans on leaving in a year; employers always lose money on training new employees. It's no different than telling an employer that you plan to leave in a year for any other reason. You would never say—or at least you'd never be hired if you did say—that you plan to leave in a few months to travel around the world, go to law school, move across the country, have a child, or stay home and work on a novel.

Many academics have difficulty saying that they're leaving academia; try to make some kind of peace with it before you get to this point of interviewing. Remember that taking a job outside the academy doesn't mean that you have to give up research, writing, and thinking. Besides, you don't know what will happen between now and next fall. Maybe you'll decide that you like your new lifestyle. Maybe there won't be any desirable jobs in your field. Maybe your tastes will change. You can't be sure. So why shoot yourself in the foot just to set yourself apart as someone with a "higher calling"?

What to say so you're not exactly lying:
- "I love college teaching, but the job market is really tight. I know that I can fulfill my love of teaching in other ways."
- "Graduate school was a once-in-a-lifetime opportunity, but I'm ready to roll up my sleeves and get some practical experience. I'm excited at the idea of working more extensively in new media, and I've designed several web pages already."

After the Interview

Now that you've survived the interview, you still can't wait around for the phone to ring. This is the time to reiterate your interest in the position by sending a thank-you note. And the kind of note you write can make or break your candidacy. A brief, well-worded, gracious note sent promptly (within twenty-four hours of your meeting) can sway an employer who is undecided about whether to give you a shot. As with cover letters, don't use a one-size-fits-all thank-you letter. If you've interviewed with four people, send them four slightly different notes. Be specific but concise; follow up on a question they asked in the interview, or mention a particular project within the company that interests you.

There's no one obvious format for thank-you letters. Depending on the corporate culture and your relationship with the interviewer, a handwritten, typed, snail-mailed, faxed, or e-mailed note could all be appropriate. E-mail followed by snail mail is always a good combination. Don't spend too much time trying to figure out the best delivery method. It's better to act quickly than to dwell on it.

What If the Interview Doesn't Go Well?

One Ph.D. went through all the steps listed above in order to interview at a company where she really wanted to work. She was prepared, confident, and ready to wow the employer with her editorial and project management skills. But five minutes into the interview, she "realized they were looking for a technical person—not me at all."

After enduring an uncomfortable discussion about her limited technical expertise, she figured she had nothing to lose and decided to turn a negative into a positive. Within a few hours of the awkward meeting, she e-mailed her interviewers to let them know that while she sensed that she wasn't a good match for the particular position they had discussed, she was still very enthusiastic about the company and had skills that would be an asset in other departments. The interviewer wrote back immediately and offered to set up an interview for her in another department that would be a better fit. Her forthrightness and her confidence in her own abilities earned her a good reference from her first interviewer, and she got the second job.

The Job Offer (or Lack Thereof)

First of all, be prepared for the possibility that all your hard work might not pay off. The good news about not being selected for a post-academic job is that, unlike in academia, you don't have to wait another year to mount a new search. So don't despair if you get a rejection letter or call from one of your target companies. Instead, try to learn as much as possible from your experience. If you're comfortable with the idea, ask the interviewer to tell you her reasons for not selecting you; you may get valuable feedback.

If, however, your hard work does turn into an offer, resist the impulse to jump for joy and scream your immediate cries of acceptance over the phone. You may have years of student loans and mountains of credit card debt, but that's all the more reason to consider the offer carefully. The moment you say "yes," you've lost all your negotiating power. Express your pleasure and enthusiasm, clarify the terms of the offer, and give the employer a timetable for getting back to him or her (anywhere from a few days to a few weeks, depending on your needs and those of the employer). Use this time to make sure this is the job you really want. If you're unsure, check with your other preferred employers. Explain your situation and inquire about the extent of their interest in you.

Negotiation

Once you've decided that this is the job for you, you still need to control your enthusiasm when talking with your future employer. Amada Wood, a graduate student in English who once worked in human resources for a large firm, advises that you use this time to negotiate a package. She was amazed, she told us, at how few people, especially women, tried to negotiate their salaries. As part of her job, she offered people less than she was prepared to pay. "If they didn't speak up for themselves, they started at lower salaries than they would've had otherwise," she recalls. Academia certainly doesn't prepare you for these kind of negotiations. Professors' salaries are rarely open to much nego tiation, even when the job market isn't tight. But you'll need to learn this skill as you enter the business world, because you can give yourself a $5,000 or $10,000 raise before you even begin work. And negotiating is so common, you'll actually look a little odd if you *don't* try to better your offer.

The tone of your negotiations should be friendly and cooperative. You're trying to work out an agreeable arrangement with the company, not grandstanding or bluffing about your enormous value as an employee. Instead, you want to present options and then keep quiet while they're being considered.

Say nothing about salary or benefits until you have a job offer in writing.

It may take awhile for the company to produce a written offer (there's often lots of legalese involved), but be patient. Assure the manager that you're very interested in working together, and you look forward to talking more specifically about these issues once you see it in writing.

Research appropriate salaries in the field.

"Graduate students simultaneously overestimate and underestimate their own worth," says John Romano, former English professor turned network television producer. "They think they could be the next Spielberg, but they don't believe me when I say it's possible to get an entry-level screenwriting job." We all suffer these wild swings of confidence. One minute you think that you deserve a vice president's salary, and the next minute you're sure you belong in the mailroom. The cure for this disease is simple: Do some research. There are numerous websites (including www.salary.com and the Bureau of Labor Statistics, www.bls.gov) that offer information on starting salaries for a variety of fields and positions. In addition, use your industry network to get a sense of what average salaries are for someone with your qualifications.

Let the employer throw out the first number.
If the employer gives you a salary range—say, $25,000 to $40,000—focus on the upper end of the range. You may, for example, want to say something like "$40,000 seems a little on the low side, but we can discuss it later." And no matter what the employer says, remember to wait for the written offer before making a commitment.

Use objective criteria.
If you decide to ask for more money, be prepared to back up your request with specific reasons. It's not enough to just say, "I want more money." It's much better to provide data indicating that the offer on the table is below average for the position in question, or that you're considering a better offer from another company for a similar position.

Learn your benefits.
Salary isn't the only thing to negotiate when you accept a job offer. Maybe you want to adjust the start date to give you an extra month to finish your dissertation, or ask for additional vacation days for an already-planned trip. Also consider negotiating relocation expenses, flexible hours, tuition assistance for relevant classes, and so on. An employer may have limits on how much s/he can pay but could have more flexibility in these areas. For example, Ph.D.'s learn quickly that a six-month salary review (instead of twelve-month) is a smart request, and one that's easy for the employer to accommodate. If you're a graduate student, you may not have much experience with benefit packages, so be sure to analyze your written offer carefully. Ask friends about what their health and other benefit packages include and how your offer compares. Benefits can be as important as salary in determining your new quality of life. Your ability to negotiate your salary, your responsibilities, and your promotion path is never stronger than before you've accepted a job offer. Don't waste this opportunity.

Adjusting to Your New Job

Once you've accepted the position, take a deep breath and get ready for your next adventure. Be prepared for some anxiety, since any transition is stressful. But know that because you've been trained to learn, you have all the skills you need to handle being the new kid on the block. Josh Fost, a Ph.D. in neurobiology who now works in consulting, remembers the shock of his first day: There was "no orientation whatsoever in the beginning; I was overwhelmed. I sat in my cube trying to be productive on a project I didn't have a clue about. I opened up the manuals, stared at the code, and three weeks later the project was done and massively successful." While his graduate school training helped him puzzle out a solution, Fost remembers feeling that he was no longer on familiar turf. He was using the same computer programs, doing similar kinds of work, but he was surrounded by an entirely different culture: "Suddenly, I'm wearing khakis!" he remembers.

A good rule to remember in your new job: Don't say or do anything rash for three months. Don't complain and don't make any suggestions. It will be tempting to suggest all kinds of "improvements" to the way things work during your first few days and weeks on the job. However, resist the impulse to speak up right away. Wait until you have a better understanding of why things are done a certain way before you open your mouth. Concentrate on asking questions and learning how things work before trying to suggest improvements. And even after your first few months on the job, it's wise to phrase your suggestions as questions—"What's the logic behind X?"—instead of complaints. Make sure your questions are sincere requests for information, rather than thinly veiled judgments. In time, you'll be able to make more informed suggestions, and your colleagues will receive them much more readily from someone who has already proved themselves as a colleague.

Whatever bumps you encounter in your first job, remember that you've just taken a first step into a new world. Few choices in life are perfect, irrevocable, or final. Give your new job a fair shot, but also remember that if you don't like it, you can always take another route.

....

POST-ACADEMIC PROFILE:
ANNIE HURLBUT, FOUNDER OF PERUVIAN CONNECTION,
A.B.D. IN ANTHROPOLOGY

As a grad student doing fieldwork in Peru in the mid-1970s, Annie Hurlbut bought a hand-knit sweater from a local market as a birthday present for her mother. When friends asked for copies, Hurlbut and her mother decided to fill the demand. Hurlbut left her Ph.D. program at the University of Illinois the following year to work on Peruvian Connection full-time. In 1999 the $35 million catalog and Internet-sales company (www.peruvianconnection.com) sold about two hundred thousand pieces of Peruvian clothing and artwork. Almost one hundred employees work for the company from her mother's Kansas farm.

In keeping with her principles, Hurlbut ensures that the Peruvian women who knit the sweaters she sells are treated fairly. She pays them "more than some lawyers and schoolteachers in Peru" and has set up two day-care centers for their children. American designers create plans based on traditional patterns, and the Peruvian knitters improvise as they choose.

Although Hurlbut's business is enormously successful, what she enjoys most is being able to "use the parts of anthropology that I adored, relating to and understanding people from different cultures, [and] my fascination for Andean textiles from the past." But she still remembers how difficult it was to leave her graduate program. Being an academic "was a very large part of my identity . . . and I couldn't help but feel as if I was a quitter who had not reached a goal."

Hurlbut's advice to other academics facing similar choices is to "follow what excites and fascinates you. The energy from doing that is the fuel that you will need to succeed at whatever you've chosen."

Conclusion

Although Carol Barash is an expert on women writers of the eighteenth century, one of her favorite books is a children's story called *The Big Step*. "It's a story—really a fairy tale—about a poor boy who wants to marry the king's daughter. The king says the boy can't marry the princess unless he can jump over the tallest tower in the kingdom," she recalls. The boy invents all sorts of devices to get over the tower—a ladder, a catapult, a lever, a pulley—and ends up discarding each one after it fails to work. When the boy sees his little dog climbing up a pile of discarded inventions, he realizes that he doesn't need to leap over the tower in a single bound—he just needs to take small steps.

"And that's what it's like to leave the academy," she says. The story illustrates her belief that when trying a new career, "there's nothing wrong with being wrong." Even a big misstep can start you in the right direction. "You just need to take the first step, and the next steps will all be easier," Barash adds. Ann Kirschner of Comma International echoes this advice, reminding job hunters that "it'll never be this hard again." Once you get your first post-academic job, "no one will ever question your ability to adapt to the business world."

Remember these alums' wise words as you begin your career exploration. Try to silence the little professor inside you who dreads being wrong. Television producer John Romano warns that the worst decisions are motivated by fear. Every choice has consequences, but they are rarely disastrous or irrevocable. He says, "Security can rule you. Security involves other risks. For most of us, we don't realize how low the stakes really are in our twenties. You go down a lot of wrong roads and still turn out okay." The best decisions, we say, are made from passion, desire, and excitement. Move toward what you love, rather than shrinking from what you fear.

Instead of worrying that you'll never find the perfect job, concentrate on building the life you want. What do you need to be happy? Where do you want to live? How do you want to spend your days? Would you like to learn something new? Do you want to return to something old? Try to take what you love about the academic world and leave the rest behind. As journalist and Ph.D. Alex Pang reminded us, "The life of the mind is highly portable."

You probably feel that being a teacher and a scholar is a calling, that no other career will fill you in exactly the same way. But our goal has been to show you that there are other ways to arrange your life. You can make a life for yourself that is as good as, or even better than, the one that you hope to enjoy in academia.

It's no accident that all the people we've introduced to you in this book are happy and successful. Maybe you think we've stacked the deck by only telling you about people who enjoy the post-academic life. Maybe you're wondering if we've overlooked all the miserable former academics. We admit that we looked for people with interesting stories to share, but we didn't censor anyone.

So why did most of the people we interviewed seem to share the same positive view of their new careers? We think it's because their post-academic lives have been shaped by the same intelligence, the same creativity, and the same desire to learn that brought them to graduate school in the first place. Intellectuals don't lose their abilities the moment they step off campus. The talents that made you successful in academia can propel you into the post-academic world. Strong, independent thinkers can't help carving out interesting careers. Success is the almost inevitable side effect of pursuing what you love.

Even if you believe us when we say that your instincts and your passion are the best career guides you can find, what does that mean for you in practical terms? If it's all about serendipity and kismet, what on earth are you supposed to do today? Remember that we haven't suggested radical changes or abrupt shifts. Instead, we've tried to get you to examine your life more closely. So all you need to do today is consider taking some small half-steps into your own undiscovered future. As Cynthia Thomiszer described her move from English professor to computer company executive, "My decision to leave academia was more of an evolution than a revolution." And that's our goal: to sow the seeds of evolution among academics.

We want to hear about your experiences. Tell us about your fears, your hopes, your mistakes, and your triumphs. Have we helped you? What did we forget to tell you? Send us an e-mail at phdfeedback@yahoo.com or visit us at www.careersforphds.com and tell us your story. We'd love to hear from you.